The New Chili Cuisine

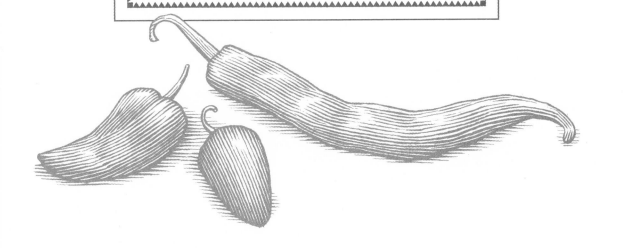

The New Chili Cuisine

100 Mouthwatering Recipes, from Mild to Wild

Nancy S. Hughes

CB

CONTEMPORARY BOOKS
A TRIBUNE COMPANY

Library of Congress Cataloging-in-Publication Data

Hughes, Nancy S.
    The new chili cuisine : 100 mouthwatering recipes,
from mild to wild / Nancy S. Hughes.
        p.   cm.
    Includes index.
    ISBN 0-8092-3191-3
    1. Chili con carne.   I. Title.
TX749.H78   1996
641.8′23—dc20   96-5915
                                       CIP

Interior design by Kim Bartko
Illustrations by Dan Krovatin

Featured on the cover: Mild Black Bean and Rice Chili with Hot Jalapeño-Lime Oil (see Index)

Published by Contemporary Books
An imprint of NTC/Contemporary Publishing Company
Two Prudential Plaza, Chicago, Illinois 60601-6790
Manufactured in the United States of America
International Standard Book Number: 0-8092-3191-3

10   9   8   7   6   5   4   3   2   1

To my husband, Greg,

my heart, my best friend, my mentor;

To my son Taft, 12, my salt and pepper,

constant, dependable, and ever present,

making everything feel just right;

To my daughter, Annie, 17, the cream in my coffee,

comforting, securing, giving a warm glow inside;

To my son Will, 20, my entire spice cabinet!

▼▼▼

Explore new territory.

Experience exotic foods and spice combinations.

Relax and capture the fullness of the flavors.

Life is full of spice, if only we would taste it.

▼▼▼

Contents
▼▼▼

6. Quick and Easy Chilies   77

Acknowledgments

▼▼▼

I want to thank my seasoned friend, Eunice Swift, for always being there to add that final touch, that final spice; Kathy and Debbie Strawn, who answer one question with 20 right suggestions; Rose Martinez of Freida's, Inc., for her tremendous help in explaining the chile market; Melissa and David Callaway, whose patience and calming mannerisms helped me find direction; Tim Deasy, who was there with his sense of humor and the right words when it got a little crazy; and my editor, Linda Gray, whose opinions are highly respected and appreciated. Her guidance and straight-forwardness keep me focused book after book.

I especially want to thank my father, Stephen J. Simko, who taught me the basics of food appreciation. The expressions on his face and his subtle and sometimes spicy comments were, and still are, the ultimate expression of appreciation! Thank you.

Introduction
▼▼▼

Chili. For most of us the word brings to mind our culinary love of all things southwestern, but chilies are not limited to our borders. Chili has grown far beyond its basic definition of stewed meats and chile peppers. Dishes of spicy peppers and small cuts of meat prepared by stewing are found throughout the world. A Moroccan meal of lamb, peppers, and spices is a chili too, in everything but name. And so it is with many other spicy dishes from all over the world.

This book contains 100 hearty, intensely flavorful chili recipes derived from regions of North, South, and Central America, Mexico and the Caribbean, the Mediterranean, the Middle East, and Asia. In addition to a wide variety of extraordinarily innovative and spicy new chilies, I've included a chapter on chile soups. These soups are perfect for lunch or as part of a hearty meal.

About Chiles

Fresh chiles have a milder flavor, dried chiles a more pronounced flavor. Different chiles possess different levels of heat, even from chile to chile in the same category, but the more pointed in shape a variety is, the hotter it is. Also, the smaller the pepper, the hotter the heat, with the exception of the habanero, or Scotch bonnet, which is the hottest chile in the world. In all cases the majority of the heat comes from the seeds and the membrane connecting the seeds to the lining of the pepper.

Use the seeds according to your preference for a mild or a hotter chili.

Using dairy products, such as sour cream or cheese, or serving milk helps cool the heat of a fiery chili. Water, tea, soft drinks, and beer are good accompaniments to chili, but they do very little to quench a chile pepper's fire. If the chiles suggested in a recipe seem too hot for your personal taste, simply combine them with a milder chile. This will cut the heat without diminishing flavor.

A Word of Caution

When handling chiles, it is highly advisable to wear rubber or plastic gloves to prevent skin burns. Disposable gloves are ideal and inexpensive. They can be purchased in pharmacies and paint stores.

Chop peppers on a nonpenetrable surface such as granite or stainless steel or simply on a ceramic plate. Be sure to thoroughly wash the knives and any other utensils used to prevent any burns.

If skin burns should occur, wash the area with soapy water and apply aloe vera gel. If the juices come in contact with the eyes, flush them with cool water or milk to neutralize the chile pepper oil.

Anaheims and poblano chiles are often roasted and peeled because their tough outer skins will separate from the meat of the pepper and float unattractively in the chili. Roasting is also an excellent way to incorporate a rich, full-bodied smoky flavor into a chili.

Fresh Chile Varieties

Anaheim

Sometimes labeled New Mexico pepper, California pepper, chile verde, Rio Grande pepper, or California green chile.

Appearance: Long, green, and tapering. The pods average 6–7 inches long and 1¼–1¾ inches in diameter.

Flavor: Mildly pungent when grown in California; hotter when grown in New Mexico.

Purchasing: Choose chiles that are firm with a good green color. May be slightly lumpy or smooth, depending on variety.

Storing: Refrigerate for about 3 weeks. Wrap in paper towels. Do not store in plastic, or they will sweat and spoil rapidly.

Preparing: Roast before chopping as desired or leave skin on and chop very fine after removing stems, seeds, and membranes.

Freezing: Roast chiles (do not peel) and wrap individually in plastic wrap to prevent them from sticking together or put them in small individual plastic sandwich bags.

Jalapeño

Appearance: Usually no more than 2 inches long and ¾ inch wide. Pointed and smooth-skinned. Bright to dark green, sometimes greenish black; also sometimes red.

Flavor: Extremely hot.

Purchasing: Choose chiles that are firm and unwrinkled, with shiny skins. Dry lines or striations are not a blemish but a sign of hotness.

Storing: Refrigerate in crisper section for up to 2 weeks, wrapped in paper towels. Do not wrap jalapeños in plastic, or they will spoil quickly.

Preparing: Wearing rubber or plastic gloves, remove stems. Remove seeds and membranes for a milder flavor.

Freezing: Simmer in water to cover for 5 minutes, drain, and freeze three or four in each plastic bag. If frozen without blanching, they lose their spicy flavor.

Poblano

Appearance: Long and tapered with a triangular shape; dark green, sometimes almost black in color.

Flavor: Spicier than green bell peppers.

Purchasing: Choose chiles that are firm and shiny.

Storing: Refrigerate in crisper section for up to 2 weeks, wrapped in paper towels. Do not wrap poblanos in plastic, or they will spoil quickly.

Preparing: If tough skin is left on, chop fine. Roast chiles for easy removal of skin and more pungent flavor.

Freezing: Simmer in water to cover for 5 minutes, drain, and freeze three or four in each plastic bag. If poblanos are frozen without blanching, they lose their spicy flavor.

Serrano

Appearance: Small and tapering, usually $1\frac{1}{2}$ inches long and $\frac{1}{2}$ inch wide. Dark green in color.

Flavor: Very hot; hotter than jalapeño chiles.

Storing: Refrigerate in crisper for up to 2 weeks, wrapped in paper towels. Do not wrap in plastic, or they will spoil quickly.

Preparing: Wearing rubber or plastic gloves, remove stems. Remove seeds and membranes for a milder flavor.

Freezing: Simmer in water to cover for 5 minutes, drain, and freeze three or four in each plastic bag. If frozen without blanching, they lose their spicy flavor.

Dried Chile Varieties

It is important to rehydrate dried chiles before adding them to other ingredients. Chiles do not rehydrate in salted water or salted stock. Without the rehydration, the desired flavors of the particular chile will not be released. Do not rehydrate more than you need for a recipe because the chiles will lose strength, flavor, and heat.

Some chiles may take longer to rehydrate than the time suggested in the recipe; the longer they have been dried, the longer they will take to rehydrate, though the flavors will still be good.

Ancho

A dried form of the poblano. Sometimes confused with *mulato*.

Appearance: Broad triangular shape, approximately 4½ inches long and 3 inches wide with a wrinkled appearance; deep mahogany in color.

Flavor: Fairly hot.

Purchasing: Can be purchased in small packages, usually found in the produce section of large supermarkets or in Latin American shops.

Storing: Keep in a cool, dry area. To avoid attracting insects, wrap chiles in plastic and store in the crisper of the refrigerator for up to 2 months.

Rehydrating: Pour 1 cup boiling water over the chiles and soak them for 2–3 minutes or until completely softened. Reserve the soaking liquid.

Preparing: Wearing rubber or plastic gloves, remove stems. Remove seeds and membranes as well for an even milder flavor. Place in a blender with the amount of water recommended in the recipe. Blend until smooth, about 2–3 minutes, and proceed as directed.

Chile de Árbol

A type of cayenne chile.

Appearance: Vibrant, orange-red, slightly curved, about 3 inches long and ½ inch wide, tapering to a sharp point; skin is smooth, rather brittle, and translucent.

Flavor: Very hot, vicious bite.

Purchasing: Can be purchased in small packages, usually found in the produce section of large supermarkets or in Asian and Latin American shops.

Storing: Keep in a cool, dry area for up to 2 months.

Preparing: Use whole chiles with stems on to add heat to a dish and then remove the chile at the end of the cooking. Be careful not to remove the stems in the process because of the intense heat of the seeds. If the chiles are to be used chopped, wear rubber gloves and remove the stems after cooking. Using the flat side of a knife, press gently and slide the knife across the chile, forcing the seeds out. Then chop the chiles and proceed as directed in the recipe.

Chipotle

Dried smoked jalapeño chiles.

Appearance: Small, elongated teardrop shape, about 2 inches long. Light to medium brown to brick red color.

Flavor: Very hot, with a distinctive smoky, meaty flavor.

Purchasing: Can be purchased in small packages, usually found in the produce section of large supermarkets or in Latin American shops.

Storing: Keep in a cool, dry place for up to 2 months.

Rehydrating: Pour 1 cup boiling water over the chiles and soak for 30 minutes or longer. Quick method: Bring 1 cup water and the chiles to a boil and boil for 5 minutes. Remove from the heat and let stand for 10 minutes longer to soften. How long the chiles have been dried will determine how long they take to rehydrate. Reserve the soaking water.

Preparing: Wearing rubber or plastic gloves, remove the stems, seeds, and membranes. Place in a blender along with the amount of water recommended in the recipe. Blend until smooth, about 2–3 minutes, and proceed as directed.

Guajillo

Sometimes labeled *mirasol, puya,* or *pullia.*

Appearance: Orange-red to brown in color with an elongated shape that tapers to a point. Usually 4–6 inches long and 1–1½ inches in diameter.

Flavor: Sweet-hot with berry overtones.

Purchasing: Can be purchased in small packages, usually found in the produce section of large supermarkets or in Latin American shops.

Storing: Keep in a cool, dry area for up to 2 months. To avoid attracting insects, wrap chiles in plastic and store in the crisper in the refrigerator.

Rehydrating: Pour 1 cup boiling water over the chiles and soak for 20–30 minutes to soften. Quick method: Bring 1 cup water and the chiles to a boil and boil for 5 minutes. Remove from the heat and let stand for 10 minutes to soften. How long the chiles have been dried will determine how long they take to rehydrate. Reserve the soaking liquid.

Preparing: Wearing rubber or plastic gloves, remove the stems. Remove the seeds and membranes as well for an even milder flavor. Place in a blender with the amount of water recommended in the recipe and blend until smooth, about 2–3 minutes. Proceed as directed.

Habanero

Sometimes labeled *Scotch bonnets.*

Appearance: Golden brown or rust colored, ½ inch in diameter and lantern-shaped.

Flavor: Extremely hot. Habaneros are the hottest chiles in the world, about 100 times hotter than the serrano and jalapeño chiles.

Purchasing: Can be purchased in small packages, usually in the produce section of large supermarkets or in Latin American shops.

Storing: Store in a cool, dry area for 6 months to a year.

Rehydrating: Soak in a bowl of hot water for about 20 minutes or blanch in boiling water for 2 minutes or until softened.

Preparing: Wearing rubber gloves, remove stems and seeds, place in a blender with amount of water recommended in the recipe, and blend until smooth, about 2–3 minutes. Proceed as directed. Or cook the chiles in the dish whole and carefully remove them at the end of cooking, keeping the stem intact.

New Mexican Red

Sometimes labeled *Anaheim*. They are often made into hanging ristras.

Appearance: Large, long, and tapered with smooth brick red to oxblood skin.

Flavor: Mild to hot. The milder versions are grown in California, the hotter versions in New Mexico.

Purchasing: Can be purchased in small packages, usually found in the produce section of large supermarkets or in Latin American shops.

Storing: Keep in a cool, dry area for up to 2 months.

Rehydrating: Soak in a bowl of hot water for 20–30 minutes. How long the chiles have been dried will determine how long they take to rehydrate. Reserve the soaking liquid.

Preparing: Wearing rubber or plastic gloves, remove the stems. Remove the seeds and membranes as well for an even milder flavor. Place in a blender with the amount of water recommended in the recipe and blend until smooth, about 2–3 minutes. Proceed as directed.

Pasilla

Sometimes labeled *chile negro*.

Appearance: Dark raisin-brown in color, narrow, elongated, wrinkled, and tapered, 5–6 inches long, 1–1½ inches wide.

Flavor: Medium-hot with fruity overtones and a slightly raisinlike aroma.

Purchasing: Can be purchased in small packages, usually found in the produce section of large supermarkets or in Latin American shops.

Storing: Keep in a cool, dry area. To avoid attracting insects, wrap chiles in plastic and store in the crisper in the refrigerator for up to 2 months.

Rehydrating: Pour 1 cup boiling water over the chiles and soak for about 20 minutes to soften. Quick method: Bring 1 cup water and the chiles to a boil and boil for 3 minutes. Remove from the heat and let stand for 3 minutes longer to soften. How long the chiles have been in the dried state will determine how long they take to rehydrate. Reserve the soaking liquid.

Preparing: Remove the stems. Remove the seeds and membranes for a milder flavor. Place in a blender with the amount of water recommended in the recipe and blend until smooth. Proceed as directed.

Mail-Order Sources

Most of the chiles called for in these recipes are available at major supermarkets or Latin American and Asian specialty food shops. Dried chiles are usually prepackaged in 3- and 4-ounce packages and can be found in the produce section. If the chiles you require for the recipes are not available at your local supermarket, speak with the produce manager. Most managers are very accommodating and should be able to order them for you through various sources. This will keep you from having to personally order a whole case of fresh chiles or even a small amount with high freight charges. You can also contact any of the the following sources and order the amount you need of the dried varieties.

Caribbean Spice Company
8 S. Church Street
Fairhope, AL 36532
(800) 990-6088

Freida's, Inc.
4465 Corporate Center Drive
Los Alamitos, CA 90720-2561
(800) 241-1771
(Dried and fresh chiles sold only by the case.)

Melissa's World Variety Produce
PO Box 21127
Los Angeles, CA 90021
(800) 588-0151
(Dried and fresh chiles sold in small amounts or by the case.)

New Mexican Connection
2833 Rhode Island N.E.
Albuquerque, NM 87110
(800) 933-2736
(Dried chiles sold in small amounts. Fresh chiles sold by the case.)

Pendery's Spices
304 E. Belknap
Fort Worth, TX 76102
(800) 533-1870
(Dried chiles sold in small amounts. Fresh chiles sold by the case.)

A Heart-Healthy Menu

The recipes marked with an asterisk are heart healthy. The use of lean cuts of meat, low-fat dairy products, and unsaturated oils makes these recipes low in saturated fats.

Diets high in saturated fats have been proved to be detrimental to cardiovascular health. By controlling the intake of saturated fats, the risk of heart disease can be substantially reduced or prevented. These designated recipes can be part of an overall program of maintaining cardiovascular health.

Note: Although we agree with the standards and goals of the American Heart Association, this book is not affiliated with the organization.

As new items of produce are becoming more and more readily available in every part of the country and our tastes expand to welcome exotic new flavors, we search for ways to put some delicious adventures into our cooking and eating. Experimenting with new combinations of ingredients opens a delectable world of cooking and dining pleasures.

Throughout this book you will find chili powder and curry powder included in many recipes. Chili powder, found in the spice section of your grocery store, is a blend of seasonings including chile peppers, cumin, oregano, garlic, and salt. Curry powder, also available in your grocer's spice section, is a blend of coriander, turmeric, cumin, fenugreek, allspice, mace, garlic, red pepper, salt, and other seasonings. Each brand of chili powder and curry powder has its own distinctive seasoning blend and, therefore, its own distinctive taste.

While the chile peppers used to make these chilies, in all their many forms, offer a variety of flavors and spices, as a key ingredient they form a common thread, a universal seasoning. And chili, in all its many forms, offers a variety of flavors and spices that truly provides a new dimension in cooking. Enjoy!

I

Beef Chilies

Mexican Beef and Hominy Chili

New Mexican, ancho, and chipotle chiles slow-simmered with beef, hominy, and spices and topped with fresh cilantro leaves.

    5 cups water
    4 dried red New Mexican chiles
    2 dried ancho chiles
    2 dried chipotle chiles
    2 pounds boneless chuck roast, cut into
        1/2-inch pieces
    2 tablespoons extra-virgin olive oil
    1 1/2 cups chopped yellow onion
    2 garlic cloves, minced
    1/2 teaspoon ground cinnamon
    1/4 teaspoon ground allspice
    1 slice white bread
    2 10-ounce cans condensed beef broth
    1 16-ounce can hominy, rinsed and
        drained

Bring 2 cups of the water to a boil. Place chiles in a bowl, cover with boiling water, and let stand for 20–30 minutes to rehydrate.

While chiles are soaking, coat a dutch oven with low-calorie cooking spray and heat over medium-high heat for 1 minute. In three separate batches, add beef, brown, and, using a slotted spoon, remove and set aside.

Add 1 tablespoon of the oil to pan drippings and heat for 1 minute. Add onion and garlic and cook for 4 minutes or until onion is translucent. Remove from heat and set aside.

Wearing rubber or plastic gloves, remove chiles from water (reserve water). Remove stems, seeds, and membranes. Place chiles, cinnamon, allspice, bread, 1/2 cup of the reserved chile water, onion, and garlic in a blender. Blend to a thick paste (about 1 minute). Over medium-high heat, heat remaining 1 tablespoon oil in dutch oven, add chile mixture, and cook, stirring with a flat spatula, for 10 minutes, being careful not to burn. Whisk in remaining chile water, remaining 3 cups water, and beef broth. Bring to a boil, add beef and hominy, and return to a boil. Reduce heat and simmer, uncovered, for 2 hours. Flavor improves if chili is refrigerated overnight or for at least 4 hours. Reheat over low heat before serving.

Makes 6–7 cups

SUGGESTED GARNISH: Cilantro sprigs

Cook's Note: Cooking the paste enhances the flavors of the chiles and other seasonings.

New Mexican Red Chili

This is a delicious example of the traditional red chili of New Mexico. Its hearty flavor comes from a combination of New Mexican red chiles, beef, onion, garlic, cumin, and oregano.

6–8 dried New Mexican red chiles
3 cups boiling water
2 tablespoons extra-virgin olive oil
2 pounds boneless chuck roast, cut into
 ¹/₂-inch pieces
1 cup finely chopped yellow onion
8 garlic cloves, minced
2 tablespoons ground cumin
1 tablespoon dried oregano leaves
2 14¹/₂-ounce cans beef broth (not
 condensed)

Place chiles in a mixing bowl, cover with boiling water, and let stand for 20 minutes to rehydrate.

While chiles are soaking, place 1 tablespoon of the oil in a dutch oven and heat over high heat for 1 minute. Add half the beef, brown quickly, and transfer to a separate bowl. Repeat with remaining oil and beef. Reduce heat to medium, add onion and garlic, and cook for 3 minutes or until onion is translucent. Add cumin and oregano and cook for 1 minute longer. Remove dutch oven from heat and set aside.

When chiles have rehydrated, remove from water (reserve water). Remove stems and, if a mild chili is desired, seeds and membranes. Wear rubber or plastic gloves while handling chiles. Place chiles in a blender, add 1 cup of the chile water, and blend until smooth (about 2–3 minutes). Place chile mixture, remaining chile water, broth, and beef and its juices in the dutch oven. Bring to a boil, reduce heat, and simmer, uncovered, for 2 hours, stirring occasionally. If a thinner chili is desired, add a small amount of water after 1¹/₂ hours of cooking. Flavors improve if chili is refrigerated overnight or for at least 4 hours. Reheat over low heat before serving.

Makes 4–5 cups

SUGGESTED GARNISH:
Finely chopped
white or yellow onion

Cattle Trail Chili with Sour Cream and Scallions

Here's a full-flavored chili, prepared with a generous amount of ground beef, sausage, and cilantro and seasoned with your favorite beer.

- 2 pounds ground chuck
- 1 pound hot Italian sausage, casings removed
- 3 cups chopped yellow onion
- 6 garlic cloves, minced
- ½ cup chili powder
- 3 tablespoons ground cumin
- 1½ tablespoons dried oregano leaves
- 2 14½-ounce cans diced tomatoes, undrained
- ¼ cup tomato paste
- 1 teaspoon sugar
- 1 12-ounce can beer (see Note)
- 2 cups water
- 1½ teaspoons salt
- 1 cup chopped fresh cilantro leaves

Heat a dutch oven (preferably cast iron) over high heat for 1 minute. Add ground chuck and sausage, brown, and, using a slotted spoon, transfer to paper towels to drain. Pour off all but 1 tablespoon of the pan drippings, reduce heat to medium-high, and add onion, garlic, chili powder, cumin, and oregano. Cook for 6–7 minutes or until edges of onions begin to brown slightly.

Add remaining ingredients except cilantro and meat and bring to a boil. Add meat and return to a boil. Reduce heat and simmer, uncovered, for 30 minutes. Remove from heat, stir in cilantro, and let stand, uncovered, for 15 minutes before serving. Flavor improves if chili is refrigerated overnight or for at least 4 hours. Reheat over medium heat before serving.

Makes about 10 cups

SUGGESTED GARNISH: Sour cream topped with chopped scallions

Cook's Note: Use a light beer such as lager. The pronounced flavor of a dark beer will overpower the other seasonings. A beer labeled *light*, meaning lower in calories, will be too weak.

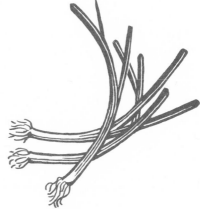

Beef Chilies 5

Heart-Stopping Chili with Beans

Pork and beef are combined with a variety of chiles to produce this richly flavored dish.

1 ounce (2 tablespoons) beef suet
2 tablespoons bacon drippings
1 pound boneless chuck, cut into ½-inch
    pieces
1 pound boneless pork shoulder, cut into
    ½-inch pieces
1½ cups chopped yellow onion
6 garlic cloves, minced
5 cups water
3 dried New Mexican red chiles
2 dried ancho chiles
1 dried pasilla chile
1 tablespoon ground cumin
1½ teaspoons dried oregano leaves
1 tablespoon flour
1 15-ounce can dark red kidney beans,
    rinsed and drained
1½ teaspoons salt
½ teaspoon black pepper

Place a dutch oven (preferably cast iron) over high heat. Add suet and bacon drippings and cook until suet just begins to brown lightly. Add half the meat, brown quickly, and, using a slotted spoon, transfer to a plate. Repeat with remaining meat.

Reduce heat to medium-high, add onion and garlic, and cook, stirring, for 3 minutes. Return meat and any accumulated juices to the dutch oven, add 2 cups of the water, and stir to blend thoroughly. Bring to a boil. Reduce heat, cover tightly, and simmer for 1 hour.

While mixture is simmering, preheat oven to 250°F. Place dried chiles on a baking sheet and bake for 3 minutes. Bring 2 cups water to a boil. Remove chiles from oven, place in a bowl, and cover with boiling water. Let stand 15 minutes to rehydrate.

Remove from water (reserve water). Remove stems and, if a mild chili is desired, seeds and membranes. Wear rubber or plastic gloves while handling chiles. Place chiles in a blender with reserved chile water and blend to a smooth paste (about 1–2 minutes).

When meat has cooked for 1 hour, add chile paste, 2 teaspoons of the cumin, and oregano. Cover tightly and simmer for 1½ hours more.

Whisk together remaining 1 cup water and flour and stir into chili. Add beans, salt, black pepper, and remaining teaspoon cumin. Simmer for 15 minutes more, uncovered. Remove from heat and let stand, uncovered, for at least 15 minutes to absorb flavors. Flavors are greatly enhanced if chili is refrigerated overnight or for at least 4 hours. Reheat over low heat.

Makes about 6 cups

Suggested garnish: Dark red kidney beans (rinsed and blotted dry with paper towels) tossed with a bit of olive oil for added flavor and an appetizing sheen. Mound a small amount of beans in the center of each serving.

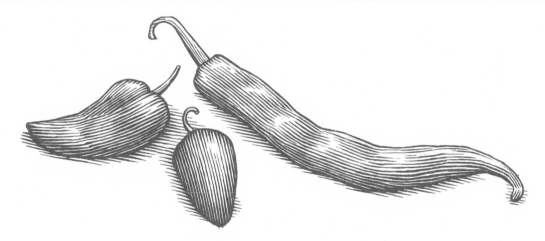

Spicy Orange Beef and Red Pepper Chili*

This chili takes on a spicy-sweet flavor as beef is cooked slowly with ginger, soy sauce, mild red peppers, and a hint of fresh orange.

1 pound boneless lean top round, cut into
   ½-inch pieces
1 teaspoon vegetable oil
1 cup chopped yellow onion
2 garlic cloves, minced
5 cups water
2 teaspoons beef bouillon granules
1 teaspoon grated fresh ginger
½ teaspoon hot red pepper flakes
1 medium red bell pepper, chopped
2 tablespoons reduced-sodium soy sauce
3 tablespoons orange juice concentrate
1¼ teaspoons sugar
3–4 cups hot cooked rice (optional)

Coat a dutch oven (preferably cast iron) with low-calorie cooking spray and heat over medium-high heat for 1 minute. Add half the beef, brown, and, using a slotted spoon, transfer to a bowl. Repeat with remaining meat.

Add oil to dutch oven, add onion and garlic, and cook over high heat for 4 minutes or until onion is translucent. Add beef and any accumulated juices, water, bouillon granules, ginger, and red pepper flakes. Bring to a boil, reduce heat, and simmer, uncovered, for 1 hour.

Add red bell pepper and soy sauce and cook for 20 minutes more. Remove from heat.

At serving time, reheat chili, remove from heat, and stir in orange juice concentrate and sugar. Let stand, uncovered, for 5 minutes before serving. Serve over rice if desired.

Makes about 4 cups

SUGGESTED GARNISH: Orange rind curls

Cook's Note: The orange juice concentrate must be added at serving time to retain the fresh orange flavor. If it is added earlier, the flavor will be flat.

Indonesian Beef Chili with Fresh Ginger and Hot Peppers

Small pieces of beef are simmered in a spicy paste of red pepper and fresh ginger, creating a high, clean heat.

- 1 tablespoon hot red pepper flakes
- 1 tablespoon salt
- 1 cup chopped yellow onion
- 4 garlic cloves, minced
- 1 2-inch slice fresh ginger, peeled and grated
- 3 plum tomatoes
- 2 pounds boneless chuck roast, cut into ½-inch pieces
- 2 tablespoons vegetable oil
- 1 quart water
- 3–4 cups hot cooked rice

Place red pepper flakes, salt, onion, garlic, ginger, and tomatoes in a blender and blend to a smooth paste (about 2 minutes).

Coat a 12-inch nonstick skillet with low-calorie cooking spray and heat over high heat for 1 minute. Add one-third of the beef and brown, stirring constantly. Using a slotted spoon, transfer to a bowl. Repeat twice more with remaining meat.

Add oil to pan drippings and heat over medium-high heat for 1 minute. Add paste and cook for 5 minutes, stirring constantly, until paste is slightly thickened and beginning to darken. Reduce heat to low, cover tightly, and simmer for 5 minutes. Add beef and any accumulated juices, and water. Stir to blend thoroughly. Bring to a boil, reduce heat, cover tightly, and simmer for 1 hour. Uncover and continue simmering for 45 minutes. The flavor improves if chili is refrigerated overnight or for at least 4 hours. Reheat over low heat before serving over rice.

Makes about 6 cups

Suggested garnish: Small fresh red jalapeños, whole or sliced, or sliced scallions

Burgundy Beef and Cracked Pepper Chili with Horseradish Sour Cream*

This is a rather sophisticated chili, enlivened by fresh jalapeños, cracked black pepper, and herbs, and served with a sour cream–horseradish sauce.

CHILI

1 tablespoon extra-virgin olive oil
1 pound boneless top sirloin, cut into
    ½-inch pieces
½ cup finely chopped yellow onion
½ cup finely chopped green bell pepper
2 garlic cloves, minced
2 fresh jalapeño chiles, seeded and
    chopped (see Note)

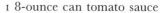

1 8-ounce can tomato sauce
1 10-ounce can condensed beef broth
1¾ cups water
2 tablespoons burgundy
½ teaspoon dried thyme leaves
1 small bay leaf
1 teaspoon cracked black pepper
1 tablespoon chili powder
1 tablespoon flour
¼ teaspoon sugar
¼ teaspoon salt or to taste
6 ounces egg noodles, cooked (makes
    about 3 cups)

HORSERADISH SOUR CREAM

⅔ cup sour cream
3 tablespoons prepared horseradish
¼ teaspoon salt or to taste
Cracked black pepper to taste
2 tablespoons chopped scallion

Make the Chili

Place oil in a dutch oven (preferably cast iron) and heat over high heat for 1 minute. Add half the beef, brown, and, using a slotted spoon, transfer to a bowl. Repeat with remaining beef.

Add onion, bell pepper, and garlic to pan drippings. Cook over medium-high heat, stirring occasionally, for 4 minutes or until edges of onion begin to brown. Add jalapeño chiles, tomato sauce, broth, 1¼ cups of the water, burgundy, thyme, bay leaf, cracked pepper, beef, and any accumulated juices. Bring to a boil. Reduce heat to low, cover tightly, and simmer for 1 hour. Add chili powder, cover tightly, and simmer for 30 minutes more.

In a small bowl, whisk together flour and remaining ½ cup water until smooth. Add to dutch oven along with sugar and salt.

Cook, stirring, until slightly thickened (2–3 minutes). Remove from heat and let stand, uncovered, for 15 minutes before serving. Flavors improve if chili is refrigerated overnight or for at least 4 hours. Reheat over low heat.

Make the Sauce

In a small bowl, combine sour cream, horseradish, and salt. Whisk together until smooth. Refrigerate until serving time. Top each serving with a dollop of sauce and sprinkle with cracked pepper and scallions.

Makes about 4 cups chili, about ¾ cup topping

Cook's Note: Wear rubber or plastic gloves while handling chiles.

Tamale Chili with Cheddar Cheese

In this substantial chili, ground beef is simmered with green chiles, tomatoes, beans, and hominy, smothered in sharp cheddar, and topped with crisp scallions. The hominy and masa harina—both corn products—give the chili the taste of tamales.

1 pound coarsely ground chuck
1 cup chopped yellow onion
1 garlic clove, minced
¼ cup chili powder
4 teaspoons ground cumin
1 teaspoon paprika
1 teaspoon dried oregano leaves
2 14½-ounce cans diced tomatoes, undrained
1 4-ounce can green chiles, rinsed and drained
1 tablespoon sugar
4½ cups water
1 15-ounce can dark red kidney or pinto beans, rinsed and drained
1 16-ounce can yellow hominy, rinsed and drained
1½ teaspoons salt
3 tablespoons masa harina (see Note)
2 cups (about ½ pound) grated sharp cheddar cheese

Heat a dutch oven (preferably cast iron) over high heat for 1 minute. Add beef, brown quickly, and, using a slotted spoon, transfer to paper towels to drain. Pour off excess grease from dutch oven, reduce heat to medium-high, and add onion and garlic. Cook for 4 minutes or until onion is translucent. Add chili powder, 1 tablespoon of the cumin, paprika, oregano, and beef and cook for 1 minute.

Add tomatoes and their liquid, green chiles, sugar, and 4 cups of the water and bring to a boil. Reduce heat to low and simmer, uncovered, for 30 minutes. Add beans, hominy, and salt and cook for 30 minutes more.

In a small bowl, whisk together masa harina and remaining ½ cup water to make a paste. Add to dutch oven along with remaining 1 teaspoon cumin. Cook for 10 minutes or until slightly thickened.

Remove from heat and let stand for 15 minutes to cool slightly. This prevents cheese from curdling when added. Add cheese and stir until completely melted. Flavors improve greatly and blend if chili is refrigerated overnight or for at least 4 hours. Reheat over low heat.

Makes 8–9 cups

SUGGESTED GARNISH: Chopped scallions

Cook's Note: Masa harina is a fine corn flour used for tortillas and tamales. It can be found in the baking section of major supermarkets.

Chili Potpie with Jalapeño-Cheese Corn Bread

This chili casserole is baked with a Mexican corn bread topping and melted cheddar cheese. Children, especially, seem to love it.

- 1 pound ground round
- 1 cup chopped yellow onion
- ½ cup chopped green bell pepper
- 2 garlic cloves, minced
- 1 14½-ounce can diced tomatoes, undrained
- 1 cup frozen yellow corn kernels
- 1 cup canned pinto beans, rinsed and drained
- 1 cup canned beef broth (not condensed)
- 2 tablespoons chili powder
- 1 tablespoon ground cumin
- ½ teaspoon dried oregano leaves
- 1 teaspoon sugar
- ¼ teaspoon cayenne pepper
- ¼ cup chopped fresh cilantro or parsley
- 1 cup plain yellow cornmeal
- ½ cup all-purpose flour
- 2 teaspoons baking powder
- ½ teaspoon baking soda
- ½ teaspoon salt
- 1¼ cups nonfat buttermilk
- 1 large egg, well beaten

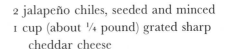

- 2 jalapeño chiles, seeded and minced
- 1 cup (about ¼ pound) grated sharp cheddar cheese

Preheat oven to 425°F. Heat a dutch oven (preferably cast iron) over high heat for 1 minute. Add beef, brown, and, using a slotted spoon, transfer to paper towels to drain. Pour off excess grease from dutch oven, reduce heat to medium-high, and add onion, green pepper, and garlic. Cook for 7–8 minutes or until edges of onion begin to brown.

Add tomatoes with their liquid, corn, beans, broth, chili powder, cumin, oregano, sugar, cayenne, cilantro, and meat and bring to a boil. Reduce heat to low, cover tightly, and simmer for 20 minutes.

In a mixing bowl, combine cornmeal, flour, baking powder, baking soda, and salt. In a separate bowl, mix together buttermilk, egg, and jalapeños. Make a well in the center of the bowl of dry ingredients and pour in the buttermilk mix. Stir gently until just blended. Spoon over chili mixture and bake, uncovered, for 25–30 minutes. Remove from oven, top with cheese, and let stand, uncovered, for 10 minutes. Reheat over low heat.

Makes about 6 cups

SUGGESTED GARNISH: Pickled jalapeño slices

Ancho-Pasilla Beef Chili

Rich and mellow ancho chiles, deep, sweet pasilla chiles, and unsweetened chocolate give this chili a satisfying, full-bodied flavor.

2¼ cups water
2 dried ancho chiles
1 dried pasilla chile
2 slices bacon
1 ounce (2 tablespoons) beef suet
2 pounds boneless chuck roast, cut into
    ½-inch pieces
1½ cups chopped yellow onion
3 garlic cloves, minced
2 14½-ounce cans beef broth (not
    condensed)
1 cup brewed coffee
½ ounce unsweetened chocolate
½ teaspoon dried oregano leaves
½ teaspoon cayenne pepper
¼ cup tomato paste

2 tablespoons flour
1 teaspoon ground cumin
3–4 cups hot cooked white rice

Preheat oven to 250°F. Bring 2 cups of the water to a boil. Place chiles on a baking sheet and bake for 3 minutes. Transfer to a bowl, pour boiling water over them, and let stand for 10–15 minutes to rehydrate.

While chiles are soaking, place bacon in a dutch oven (preferably cast iron) and cook over medium-high heat until crisp. Remove bacon, drain on a paper towel, crumble, and set aside.

Add suet to drippings in the dutch oven and increase heat to high. Add half the beef, brown, and, using a slotted spoon, transfer to a separate bowl. Repeat with remaining beef.

Reduce heat to medium. Add onion and garlic to dutch oven and cook for 4 minutes or until onion is translucent. Remove dutch oven from heat and set aside, discarding suet.

When chiles have rehydrated, remove from water (reserve water). Remove stems, seeds, and membranes. Wear rubber or plastic gloves while handling chiles. Place chiles and 1 cup of the chile water in a blender and blend until completely smooth (2–3 minutes).

Place chile paste, remaining chile water, and 3 cups broth in the dutch oven. Bring to a boil over high heat, add beef and any accumulated juice, and return liquid to a boil, scraping bottom and sides of pot with a flat spatula.

Reduce heat to low and simmer, covered, for 1½ hours. Add coffee, chocolate, oregano, cayenne, tomato paste, remaining broth, and crumbled bacon. Increase heat to medium-high and return to a boil.

Reduce heat, cover tightly, and simmer for 1 hour.

In a small bowl, combine remaining ¼ cup water, flour, and cumin and whisk until smooth. Add to beef mixture and simmer, uncovered, for 5 minutes more or until thickened. Remove chili from heat and let stand, uncovered, for 15 minutes before serving. Flavors blend and mellow if chili is refrigerated overnight or for at least 4 hours. Reheat over low heat and serve over white rice.

Makes about 6 cups

SUGGESTED GARNISH: Dollop of sour cream sprinkled with cumin and topped with chopped scallions

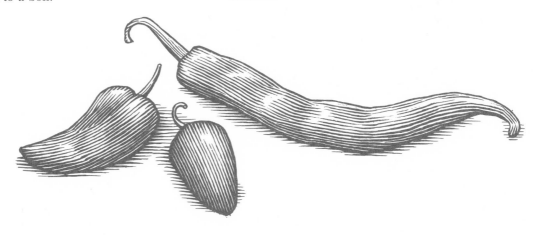

Border Beef Chili

The addition of coffee and unsweetened chocolate gives this chili its mouthwatering rich flavor.

2 tablespoons vegetable oil

2 pounds boneless chuck roast, cut into ½-inch pieces

2 cups chopped yellow onion

8 garlic cloves, minced

2 14½-ounce cans beef broth (not condensed)

2 cups water

1 cup brewed coffee

1 14½-ounce can diced tomatoes, undrained

1 8-ounce can tomato sauce

¼ cup chili powder

1 tablespoon plus 1 teaspoon ground cumin

½ ounce unsweetened chocolate

½ teaspoon ground coriander

½ teaspoon cayenne pepper

1 cup chopped green bell pepper

1 cup diced carrot

1 cup diced white potato

½ cup chopped celery

1 15-ounce can dark red kidney beans, rinsed and drained (optional)

1½ teaspoons salt

Black pepper to taste

2 tablespoons flour

¼ cup fresh chopped parsley

Place oil in a dutch oven (preferably cast iron) and heat over high heat for 1 minute. Add half the beef, brown quickly, and, using a slotted spoon, transfer to a bowl. Reduce heat to medium, add onion and garlic to pan drippings, and cook for 5–6 minutes, until edges of onion begin to brown. Add broth, water, coffee, tomatoes and their liquid, tomato sauce, and beef with any accumulated juices. Bring to a boil, reduce heat, and simmer, uncovered, for 1 hour.

Add chili powder, cumin, chocolate, coriander, and cayenne pepper. Cover and simmer for 1 hour.

Add bell pepper, carrot, potato, celery, beans (if desired), salt, and pepper. Whisk together ¼ cup water with 2 tablespoons flour and stir into chili. Bring to a boil, reduce heat, and simmer, covered, for 30 minutes. Remove from heat, add parsley, and let stand, covered, for at least 15 minutes before serving. Flavors mellow and blend if chili is refrigerated overnight or for at least 4 hours. Reheat over low heat.

Makes about 11 cups

SUGGESTED GARNISH: Chopped parsley or parsley sprigs

2

Lamb Chilies

Cincinnati-Style Five-Way Chili

This chili is a long-standing tradition in Cincinnati. Slightly sweet, slightly spicy, it's prepared with beans, served on a bed of pasta, and topped with grated cheese and finely chopped onion.

1 pound ground lamb or chuck
1 cup chopped yellow onion
1½ cups chopped green bell pepper
2 garlic cloves, minced
2 tablespoons chili powder
1½ teaspoons ground cumin
1 teaspoon ground cinnamon
1 teaspoon paprika
½ teaspoon dried oregano leaves
¼ teaspoon ground allspice
¼ teaspoon ground nutmeg
½ teaspoon sugar
1 14½-ounce can diced tomatoes, undrained
½ cup water
½ ounce unsweetened chocolate
½ teaspoon Worcestershire sauce
1 15-ounce can dark red kidney or pinto beans, rinsed and drained
Salt to taste
Black pepper to taste
½ pound spaghetti, cooked (about 4 cups)
½ cup (about 2 ounces) shredded sharp cheddar or Monterey Jack cheese
¼ cup finely chopped red onion

Heat a dutch oven (preferably cast iron) over medium-high heat for 1 minute. Add meat and brown. Add onion, green pepper, and garlic and cook for 4 minutes or until onion is translucent. Add chili powder, cumin, cinnamon, paprika, oregano, allspice, nutmeg, and sugar and cook for 1 minute more.

Add tomatoes with their liquid, water, chocolate, and Worcestershire sauce and bring to a boil. Reduce heat, cover tightly, and simmer for 30 minutes. Uncover and cook for 30 minutes longer.

Remove from heat and stir in beans and salt and pepper. Cover and let stand for 15 minutes before serving over spaghetti. Top with cheese and red onion. The flavor improves if chili is refrigerated overnight or for at least 4 hours. Reheat over low heat before serving over pasta.

Makes about 4 cups

Cook's Note: "Two-way" chili contains no beans and is served over spaghetti with no topping, "three-way" adds grated cheese, "four-way" adds chopped onion, and "five-way" includes the kidney beans.

Anaheim Black Bean Lamb Chili with Cilantro

Green chiles, diced tomato, and black beans imbue this beef chili with a mild, appealing flavor and aroma.

1 tablespoon extra-virgin olive oil
1 pound lamb or beef stew meat, cut into ½-inch pieces
1 14½-ounce can diced tomatoes, undrained
2 fresh Anaheim or New Mexican green or poblano chiles, chopped fine (see Note)
1 tablespoon chili powder
1 14½-ounce can beef broth (not condensed)
2 cups water
4 garlic cloves, minced
½ teaspoon Worcestershire sauce
½ teaspoon A.1. steak sauce
2 15-ounce cans black beans, rinsed and drained
3–4 cups hot cooked white or yellow Spanish-seasoned rice (optional)

Place 1½ teaspoons of the oil in a dutch oven (preferably cast iron) and heat over high heat for 1 minute. Add half the lamb, brown quickly, and, using a slotted spoon, transfer to a bowl. Brown remaining lamb in remaining oil.

Return meat to dutch oven and add tomatoes and their liquid, green chiles, chili powder, broth, water, garlic, Worcestershire, and A.1. sauce. Bring to a boil, reduce heat, and simmer, covered, for 30 minutes.

Add beans, increase heat to high, and return to a boil. Reduce heat and simmer, uncovered, for 10 minutes. Flavors improve if chili is refrigerated overnight or for at least 4 hours. Reheat over low heat before serving over white or yellow Spanish-seasoned rice if desired.

Makes about 6 cups

SUGGESTED GARNISH:
Cilantro leaves

Cook's Note: Anaheims are usually roasted and peeled, both to impart a rich smoky flavor and to keep the tough skins from separating from the flesh and floating unattractively in the chili. When they are finely chopped, however, the skins will not be noticeable, and the additional seasonings provide a small amount of smoky taste.

Five-Spice Lamb Chili with Sweet Red Peppers

An exotic chili rich in the flavors of Asia, this dish is seasoned with sherry and sweet and hot peppers.

    2 tablespoons vegetable oil
    2 pounds lamb or beef stew meat, cut into
        ½-inch pieces
    2 cups thinly sliced yellow onion
    1 red bell pepper, cut into matchsticks
    4 garlic cloves, minced
    5 cups water
    ⅔ cup reduced-sodium soy sauce
    ¼ cup dry sherry
    1 tablespoon five-spice powder (see Note)
    ¼–½ teaspoon hot red pepper flakes
    3–4 cups hot cooked rice

Place 1 tablespoon of the oil in a dutch oven (preferably cast iron) and heat over high heat for 1 minute. Add half the lamb, brown quickly, and, using a slotted spoon, transfer to paper towels to drain. Repeat with remaining oil and lamb.

Return lamb to dutch oven and add onion, bell pepper, garlic, water, soy sauce, sherry, five-spice powder, and red pepper flakes. Bring to a boil over high heat. Reduce heat, cover tightly, and simmer for 1½ hours. For a thicker consistency, whisk 1½ teaspoons cornstarch with 2 tablespoons water, add to the chili, and cook 2–3 minutes longer or until slightly thickened. Flavors will be at their peak if chili is served immediately. Serve over rice.

Makes about 6 cups

Suggested garnish: Red bell pepper strips

Cook's Note: Five-spice powder is available at Asian markets and in many supermarkets. This Chinese ingredient is usually a blend of ground fennel, star anise, cloves, cinnamon, and peppercorns.

Lamb Chili with Dried Fruits and Burgundy

This is a Morrocan-style chili, rich in flavor with ancho peppers, dried prunes, and dried apricots, served over steaming white rice.

2 dried ancho chiles

2 cups boiling water

2 tablespoons vegetable oil

1 pound lamb stew meat, cut into ½-inch pieces

1 cup chopped yellow onion

2 garlic cloves, minced

1 14½-ounce can beef broth (not condensed)

1 cup burgundy

6 dried pitted prunes, diced

4 dried apricots, diced

1 small bay leaf

½ teaspoon dried thyme leaves

1½ teaspoons ground cumin

½ teaspoon salt or to taste

¼ teaspoon cayenne pepper

¼ teaspoon black pepper

3–4 cups hot cooked white rice

Place ancho chiles in a mixing bowl, cover with boiling water, and let stand for 10 minutes to rehydrate.

While chiles are soaking, place 1 tablespoon oil in a dutch oven (preferably cast iron) and heat over medium-high heat for 1 minute. Add half the lamb, brown, and, using a slotted spoon, transfer to a plate. Repeat with remaining oil and lamb. Add onion and garlic to pan drippings and cook for 4 minutes or until onion is translucent. Remove dutch oven from heat.

When chiles have rehydrated, remove from water (reserve water). Remove stems, seeds, and membranes, place in a blender with 1 cup of the reserved water, and blend until smooth. Wear rubber or plastic gloves while handling chiles. Place paste in dutch oven and add remaining ingredients, including lamb and any accumulated juices and remaining chile water. Bring to a boil over high heat.

Reduce heat and simmer uncovered for 1 hour and 15 minutes. Remove from heat and, if too thick, add ½ cup hot water. Let stand for at least 20 minutes before serving. Reheat over low heat before serving over rice.

Makes about 4 cups

SUGGESTED GARNISH: Strips of dried apricots and prunes with diagonally sliced scallions

Ethiopian Red Dish Chili

Distinctively seasoned, this unusual chili's flavor is an appetizing combination of rich butter, fresh ginger, and garam masala, a blend of Indian spices.

- 1 tablespoon plus 1 teaspoon butter
- 1 teaspoon grated fresh ginger
- 1 teaspoon grated garlic
- 2 tablespoons vegetable oil
- 1 pound lamb or beef stew meat, cut into ½-inch pieces
- 1 cup chopped yellow onion
- 1 14½-ounce can diced tomatoes, undrained
- 1 cup water
- 1 15-ounce can garbanzo beans, rinsed and drained, if desired
- 2 teaspoons garam masala (see Note)
- ½ teaspoon ground coriander
- ¼ teaspoon cayenne pepper

Place butter, ginger, and garlic in a small bowl and set aside to soften at room temperature. Meanwhile, place 1 tablespoon of the oil in a dutch oven (preferably cast iron) and heat over high heat for 1 minute. Add half the lamb, brown quickly, and, using a slotted spoon, transfer to paper towels to drain. Repeat with remaining oil and lamb.

Return lamb to dutch oven and add onion, tomatoes and their liquid, and water. Bring to a boil, reduce heat, and simmer, covered, for 45 minutes.

While lamb is simmering, use the back of a spoon to mash the ginger and garlic thoroughly into the butter. Set aside.

When lamb has cooked for 45 minutes, add garbanzo beans, if desired, garam masala, coriander, and cayenne and mix gently but thoroughly. Simmer, uncovered, for 30 minutes. Remove from heat and let stand uncovered for 10 minutes. Reheat over low heat.

Makes about 6 cups

SUGGESTED GARNISH: Dried chile de árbol or fresh whole red jalapeño chiles

Cook's Note: Garam masala is a classic Indian blend of aromatic spices. It usually includes coriander, cumin, ginger, black pepper, cinnamon, pimiento, cardamom, bay leaf, cloves, and nutmeg. It is sold in specialty food shops, particularly Indian.

Lamb and White Bean Chili with Tomatoes and Fennel

A true "comfort dish," this chili blends the mild flavors of lamb, Great Northern beans, and tomatoes with aromatic fresh garlic, scallions, and a variety of herbs.

2 tablespoons extra-virgin olive oil

1 pound lamb or pork stew meat, cut into ½-inch pieces

1 cup chopped yellow onion

2 garlic cloves, minced

3 cups chicken or beef broth (not condensed)

1 14½-ounce can diced tomatoes, undrained

½ cup chopped scallion

½ teaspoon dried thyme leaves

1 small bay leaf

¼ teaspoon fennel seeds

¼ teaspoon hot red pepper flakes

1 15-ounce can Great Northern beans, rinsed and drained

Place 1 tablespoon of the oil in a dutch oven (preferably cast iron) and heat over medium-high heat for 1 minute. Add half the lamb, brown, and, using a slotted spoon, transfer to paper towels to drain. Repeat with remaining lamb.

Return lamb to dutch oven, add onion and garlic, and cook for 2 minutes. Add broth, tomatoes and their liquid, scallion, thyme, bay leaf, fennel seeds, and red pepper flakes and bring to a boil.

Reduce heat, cover tightly, and simmer for 50 minutes. Add beans and cook, uncovered, for 5 minutes more. Remove from heat, gently stir in remaining tablespoon of oil, and let stand, uncovered, for 5 minutes. Flavors improve if chili is refrigerated overnight or for at least 4 hours. Reheat over low heat before serving.

Makes about 6 cups

SUGGESTED GARNISH: Chopped fresh tomatoes tossed with chopped fresh parsley

Cook's Note: Adding the oil at the end of the cooking gives the dish a richer flavor that would otherwise be lost.

Red-Wined Lamb Chili with Rosemary

Browned lamb is simmered in soy sauce, red wine, fresh garlic, green peppers, rosemary, and beef broth and served on a spicy bed of jalapeño rice.

2 tablespoons vegetable oil

2 pounds lamb or pork stew meat, cut into ½-inch pieces

1½ cups chopped green bell pepper

1 cup chopped yellow onion

4 garlic cloves, minced

2 tablespoons reduced-sodium soy sauce

2 tablespoons dry red wine

¾ teaspoon dried rosemary leaves

2 14½-ounce cans beef broth (not condensed)

½ teaspoon cayenne pepper

2 cups water

1 tablespoon flour

1½ teaspoons ground cumin

2–3 cups hot cooked rice

1–2 fresh jalapeño chiles, seeded and minced (see Note)

Place 1 tablespoon of the oil in a dutch oven (preferably cast iron) and heat over high heat for 1 minute. Add half the lamb, brown quickly, and, using a slotted spoon, transfer to a bowl. Brown remaining lamb in remaining oil.

Return lamb to dutch oven and add green pepper, onion, garlic, soy sauce, wine, rosemary, broth, and cayenne. Bring to a boil. Reduce heat, cover tightly, and simmer for 30 minutes.

In a small bowl, whisk together ¼ cup of the water and flour. Add to dutch oven along with remaining water and return to a boil. Reduce heat to low, cover tightly, and simmer for 1 hour more. Remove from heat, stir in cumin, and let stand, uncovered, for 15 minutes. Flavors improve if chili is refrigerated overnight or for at least 4 hours. Reheat over low heat. Serve over rice tossed with minced jalapeño chiles.

Makes about 4 cups

SUGGESTED GARNISH: Small whole green jalapeño chiles

Cook's Note: Use rubber or plastic gloves when mincing chile peppers. The juices can quickly be absorbed into the skin, causing it to burn.

Middle Eastern Nine-Spice Chili with Couscous

This tempting chili combines an aromatic curry of multiple spices and herbs with lamb and onions and is served over hot couscous or rice.

2 tablespoons vegetable oil
2 pounds lamb or beef stew meat, cut into
  ½-inch pieces
2 cups chopped yellow onion
½ teaspoon ground coriander
½ teaspoon ground cumin
½ teaspoon ground cinnamon
½ teaspoon ground allspice
½ teaspoon ground nutmeg
½ teaspoon ground ginger
½ teaspoon ground cardamom
½ teaspoon cayenne pepper
1 teaspoon salt
6 cups water
3–4 cups hot cooked couscous or rice

Place oil in a dutch oven (preferably cast iron) and heat over high heat for 1 minute. Add one-third of the lamb, brown, and, using a slotted spoon, transfer to a bowl. Repeat twice more with remaining meat.

Return meat plus any accumulated juices to dutch oven with onion and remaining ingredients except water and couscous. Cook over medium-high heat for 3 minutes. Add water and bring to a boil. Reduce heat and simmer, uncovered, for 1½ hours, stirring occasionally. Remove from heat. Let stand, uncovered, for 15 minutes before serving. Flavors improve if chili is refrigerated overnight or for at least 4 hours. Reheat over low heat. Serve over couscous or rice.

Makes about 5–6 cups

SUGGESTED GARNISH:
Finely chopped red
onion

3

Pork Chilies

Classic Hot New Mexican Green Chili

New Mexico has given us many incredible traditional chilies. This one boasts roasted Anaheim chiles, slow-cooked with pork and onions and seasoned with a hint of cumin.

8–10 fresh Anaheim or New Mexican
    green chiles
2 tablespoons vegetable oil
2 pounds boneless pork shoulder, cut into
    ½-inch pieces
3 cups chopped yellow onion
6 garlic cloves, minced
3 cups canned chicken broth (not
    condensed)
2½ cups water
2 medium-size ripe tomatoes, chopped
1 teaspoon salt or to taste
1 teaspoon ground cumin

Preheat broiler. Place chiles on a foil-lined oven rack and broil 2–3 inches from heat source for 10–12 minutes or until completely blistered, turning occasionally. Place in a bowl of ice water and let stand for 5 minutes.

While chiles are soaking, place oil in a dutch oven (preferably cast iron) and heat over medium-high heat for 1 minute. Add half the pork, brown, and, using a slotted spoon, transfer to a separate bowl. Repeat with remaining meat.

Reduce heat to medium, add onion and garlic to dutch oven, and cook for 4 minutes or until onion is translucent. Add broth and water and set aside.

Remove chiles from ice water, peel, and remove stems, seeds, and membranes. Finely chop chiles, add to pot, increase heat to high, and bring to a boil, scraping bottom and sides of pot. Add tomatoes, meat, and any accumulated juices and return to a boil. Reduce heat, cover tightly, and simmer for 1½ hours. Add salt and cumin, cover, and cook for 30 minutes more. Flavors improve greatly and mellow if chili is refrigerated overnight or for at least 4 hours. Reheat over low heat.

Makes about 6 cups

SUGGESTED GARNISH:
Grated Monterey
Jack cheese

Mexican Pozole*

Red chiles, pork, and onion are combined with yellow hominy to give this chili the subtle "comfort food" taste of homemade tamales.

4 dried New Mexican red chiles
2 cups boiling water
1 tablespoon vegetable oil
1½ pounds boneless lean pork, cut into
    ½-inch pieces
2 cups chopped yellow onion
6 garlic cloves, minced
2 14½-ounce cans chicken broth (not
    condensed)
1 teaspoon dried oregano leaves
½ teaspoon ground cumin
2 16-ounce cans yellow hominy, rinsed and
    drained
Salt to taste
Black pepper to taste
Chopped fresh cilantro leaves

Preheat oven to 250°F. Place chiles on a baking sheet and bake for 3 minutes. Immediately transfer to a mixing bowl, cover with boiling water, and let stand for at least 20 minutes to rehydrate.

While chiles are soaking, place oil in a dutch oven (preferably cast iron) and heat over medium-high heat for 1 minute.

Add half the pork, brown, and, using a slotted spoon, transfer to a separate bowl. Repeat with remaining pork. Add onion and garlic to dutch oven and cook for 5 minutes or until edges of onion begin to brown. Remove dutch oven from heat.

When chiles are rehydrated, remove from water (reserve water). Wear rubber or plastic gloves while handling chiles. Remove stems, seeds, and membranes and place chiles in a blender with 1 cup of the chile water. Blend until smooth (2–3 minutes).

Add chile paste to dutch oven along with remaining chile water, broth, oregano, cumin, meat, and any accumulated juices. Bring to a boil. Reduce heat to low, cover tightly, and simmer for 30 minutes. Add hominy and cook, covered, for 30 minutes more. Remove from heat, add salt and pepper, and let stand, uncovered, for 30 minutes to thicken slightly. Flavors blend if chili is refrigerated overnight or for at least 4 hours. At serving time, reheat over low heat and top with cilantro.

Makes about 8 cups

Navajo Pozole with Green Chiles

Roasted green chiles, hominy, and coriander-seasoned pork make this a perfect choice for hearty appetites.

- 4 fresh Anaheim or New Mexican green chiles
- 2 tablespoons extra-virgin olive oil
- 2 pounds boneless pork shoulder, cut into ½-inch pieces
- 1 cup chopped yellow onion
- 4 garlic cloves, minced
- 4 plum tomatoes, chopped
- ½ teaspoon cayenne pepper
- 1 quart canned chicken broth (not condensed)
- 2 cups water
- 1 16-ounce can yellow hominy, rinsed and drained
- ½ teaspoon dried oregano leaves
- ½ teaspoon ground coriander
- ½ teaspoon salt
- 1 tablespoon ground cumin

Preheat broiler. Place chiles on a foil-lined oven rack and broil 2–3 inches from heat source for 10–12 minutes or until completely blistered, turning occasionally. Immediately place chiles in a bowl of ice water and let stand for 5 minutes. Remove stems, seeds, and membranes. Chop and set aside. Wear rubber or plastic gloves while handling chiles.

Place 1 tablespoon of the oil in a dutch oven (preferably cast iron) and heat over high heat for 1 minute. Add half the pork, brown, and, using a slotted spoon, transfer to a separate plate. Repeat with remaining meat.

Reduce heat to medium, add onion and garlic, and cook for 3 minutes or until edges of onion begin to brown. Add chiles, tomatoes, cayenne, broth, and water and bring to a boil. Add meat and any accumulated juices and return to a boil.

Reduce heat to low and simmer, uncovered, for 1 hour. Add hominy, oregano, coriander, and salt, cover tightly, and simmer for 1 hour. Remove from heat, stir in cumin and remaining tablespoon of oil, and let stand, uncovered, for 20 minutes before serving. Flavors mellow and blend if chili is refrigerated overnight or for at least 4 hours. Reheat over low heat.

Makes about 6 cups

SUGGESTED GARNISH: Thin strips of roasted green chile

Italian Green Pepper Chili

This is a savory, thick white bean and tender green pepper chili with mild sausage, hot chiles, and fennel.

- 1 pound mild Italian sausage, casings removed
- 3 medium green bell peppers, chopped
- 1 cup chopped yellow onion
- 7 cups water
- 1 tablespoon chicken bouillon granules
- ½ teaspoon hot red pepper flakes
- ¼ teaspoon fennel seeds
- 2 15-ounce cans navy beans, rinsed and drained
- 1 teaspoon salt

Heat a dutch oven (preferably cast iron) over medium-high heat for 1 minute. Add sausage, brown, and, using a slotted spoon, transfer to paper towels to drain. Add peppers and onion to any pan drippings, and cook for 15 minutes or until peppers are tender. Add water, bouillon granules, red pepper flakes, and fennel. Bring to a boil, return sausage to pot, and bring back to a boil.

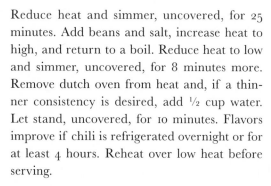

Reduce heat and simmer, uncovered, for 25 minutes. Add beans and salt, increase heat to high, and return to a boil. Reduce heat to low and simmer, uncovered, for 8 minutes more. Remove dutch oven from heat and, if a thinner consistency is desired, add ½ cup water. Let stand, uncovered, for 10 minutes. Flavors improve if chili is refrigerated overnight or for at least 4 hours. Reheat over low heat before serving.

Makes about 8 cups

Suggested garnish: Freshly grated Parmesan cheese

Fresh Tomatillo and Roasted Poblano Chili with Pork

Tiny green tomatillos and roasted poblano chiles are slow-cooked with browned pork, onions, and herbs for a chili that's slightly spicy. The addition of olive oil just before serving mellows the flavor— and the heat—of this dish.

- 6 poblano chiles
- 1 pound (about 16 small) fresh tomatillos
- 6 cups water
- 3 tablespoons extra-virgin olive oil

2 pounds boneless pork shoulder, cut into
  ½-inch pieces
2 cups chopped yellow onion
3 garlic cloves, minced
1 14½-ounce can chicken broth (not
  condensed)
2 teaspoons ground cumin
1 teaspoon dried
  oregano leaves
1 teaspoon ground
  coriander
Salt to taste

Preheat broiler. Place chiles on a foil-lined oven rack and broil 2–3 inches from heat source for 10–12 minutes or until completely blistered, turning occasionally.

While peppers are charring, remove papery skin from tomatillos and rinse them well. Bring water to a boil and add tomatillos. Return to a boil, reduce heat, and simmer, uncovered, for 8 minutes or until translucent. Drain, reserving 2½ cups liquid.

When chiles are completely blistered, immediately transfer to a bowl of ice water and let stand for 5 minutes. Remove from water (discard water) and peel. Remove stems, seeds, and

membranes. Wear rubber or plastic gloves while handling chiles. Chop and set aside.

Place 1 tablespoon of the oil in a dutch oven (preferably cast iron) and heat over medium-high heat for 1 minute. Add half the pork, brown, and, using a slotted spoon, transfer to a separate plate. Repeat with another tablespoon of oil and remaining meat.

Add onion, garlic, and chopped chiles to dutch oven and cook for 4 minutes or until onion is translucent. Add broth, cumin, oregano, coriander, meat, any accumulated juices, and 2 cups tomatillo water. Bring to a boil. Reduce heat, cover tightly, and simmer for 1 hour and 45 minutes, stirring occasionally. If too thick, add reserved ½ cup liquid. Add salt and stir in remaining tablespoon of olive oil. Let stand, uncovered, for 15 minutes before serving. Flavors greatly mellow and blend if chili is refrigerated overnight or for at least 4 hours. Reheat over medium heat.

Makes about 6 cups

SUGGESTED GARNISH: Sour
cream, diced tomatoes,
and cilantro leaves

Jamaican Habanero Pork Chili with Fresh Mango

A hot, exotic blend of pork, habanero chiles, sweet spices, and a hint of rum. The fire of this island chili is cooled with a topping of fresh mango slices.

1 very ripe medium-size fresh mango
2 tablespoons vegetable oil
2 pounds boneless pork shoulder, cut into
    ½-inch pieces
1 cup finely chopped yellow onion
½ cup chopped green bell pepper
1 teaspoon ground coriander
1½ teaspoons allspice
1½ teaspoons ground cinnamon
½ teaspoon ground nutmeg
6 cups water
2 tablespoons tomato paste
1 tablespoon A.1. steak sauce
1–2 dried habanero chiles
3 ounces (about ⅓ cup) raisins
1 teaspoon salt
2 tablespoons rum (optional)
3–4 cups hot cooked rice

Peel mango, cut in half and discard pit, slice one half, and finely chop the other half. Cover with plastic wrap and set aside.

Place 1 tablespoon of the oil in a dutch oven (preferably cast iron) and heat over high heat for 1 minute. Add half the pork, brown quickly, and, using a slotted spoon, transfer to a separate bowl. Repeat with remaining oil and pork.

Reduce heat to medium. Add onion and green pepper to pan drippings and cook for 4 minutes or until onion is translucent. Add coriander, allspice, 1 teaspoon of the cinnamon, and nutmeg. Cook for 1 minute, being careful not to burn spices. Add water, tomato paste, A.1. sauce, dried chiles, raisins, chopped mango, and pork with any accumulated juices. Bring to a boil.

Reduce heat and simmer, uncovered, for 1 hour. Add salt and stir vigorously to break up the chile. Continue simmering, uncovered, for 30 minutes more. Remove from heat and stir in remaining ½ teaspoon cinnamon and rum. Let stand, uncovered, for 20–25 minutes. Flavors will be more pronounced if chili is served immediately; flavors will blend if chili is refrigerated overnight or for at least 4 hours. Reheat over medium heat. Spoon chili over rice and top with mango slices.

Makes about 5 cups

Cook's Note: Adding the whole dried habanero(s) without rehydrating and seeding imparts additional heat and flavor. Do not add salt earlier in the cooking process. It will prevent the chile from rehydrating and softening.

Hot Sausage, White Bean, and Tomato Chili

This chili captures the rich flavors of the Old World with spicy sausage, zesty peppers, tomatoes, and tender white beans.

½ pound (about 1 cup) dried navy beans
2 quarts water
1 pound hot Italian sausage, casings
    removed (mild sausage may be
    substituted if desired)
1 cup chopped yellow onion
1 cup chopped green bell pepper
1 14½-ounce can chicken broth (not
    condensed)
1 14½-ounce can diced tomatoes,
    undrained
1 teaspoon dried oregano leaves
¼ teaspoon black pepper
Salt to taste

Place beans in a dutch oven (preferably cast iron), cover with 1 quart water, and soak overnight. Or bring to a boil, boil for 2 minutes, remove from heat, and let stand for 1 hour. Drain in a colander and set aside.

Heat dutch oven over medium-high heat for 1 minute. Add sausage and brown. Using a slotted spoon, transfer to paper towels to drain.

Return sausage to pot along with remaining ingredients, except salt, and bring to a boil. Reduce heat and simmer, uncovered, for 1½ hours. Add salt and let stand, uncovered, for 10–15 minutes. Flavors improve if chili is refrigerated overnight or for at least 4 hours. Reheat over low heat before serving.

Makes about 6 cups

Suggested garnish:
Grated mozzarella or
Parmesan cheese

Cook's Note: Do not
add salt during the cooking,
since it will toughen the beans and
prevent them from softening.

Sausage, Sun-Dried Tomato, and Wild Rice Chili

Mild Italian sausage, rich sun-dried tomatoes, and dark red kidney beans are combined with wild and white rice and chili seasonings for an authentic Italian taste.

- 1 4-ounce box wild rice
- 9 cups water
- 1 3-ounce package sun-dried tomatoes
- 1 tablespoon extra-virgin olive oil
- 1 pound mild Italian sausage, casings removed
- 1 cup chopped yellow onion
- ½ cup chopped green bell pepper
- ½ teaspoon dried basil leaves
- 1 tablespoon chili powder
- ½ teaspoon ground cumin
- ¼ teaspoon hot red pepper flakes
- 1 15-ounce can dark red kidney beans, rinsed and drained
- ¼ cup white rice
- 1¼ teaspoons salt

Cook wild rice according to package directions, drain, and set aside.

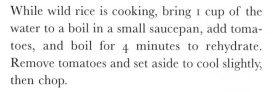

While wild rice is cooking, bring 1 cup of the water to a boil in a small saucepan, add tomatoes, and boil for 4 minutes to rehydrate. Remove tomatoes and set aside to cool slightly, then chop.

Place oil in a dutch oven (preferably cast iron) and heat over medium-high heat for 1 minute. Add sausage, brown, and, using a slotted spoon, transfer to paper towels to drain. Add tomatoes to dutch oven along with onion, green pepper, basil, chili powder, cumin, red pepper flakes, 5 cups of the remaining water, and sausage. Bring to a boil, scraping bottom with a flat spatula.

Reduce heat and simmer, uncovered, for 30 minutes. Add beans, white rice, salt, and remaining 3 cups water. Increase heat to high and bring to a boil. Reduce heat, cover tightly, and simmer for 20 minutes more. Add reserved wild rice. For a thicker consistency, let stand, uncovered, for 20 minutes. Reheat over medium-low heat before serving. Flavors will be at their peak if chili is served immediately.

Makes about 8 cups

Suggested garnish: Chopped rehydrated sun-dried tomatoes and chopped parsley

Jambalaya Chili with Shrimp

More South for your mouth! This chili is flavored with hearty kielbasa sausage, fruity poblano chiles, and hot pepper sauce.

- 6 ounces kielbasa sausage, diced (turkey kielbasa may be substituted if desired) (see Note)
- 1 cup chopped yellow onion
- 1 cup finely chopped fresh poblano chile or chopped green bell pepper
- ½ cup chopped celery
- 4 garlic cloves, minced
- ½ teaspoon dried thyme leaves
- 2 small bay leaves
- 2 cups canned chicken broth (not condensed)
- 1 quart water
- 6 ounces cooked lean ham, diced
- 1 14½-ounce can diced tomatoes, undrained
- ½ cup converted rice
- 1 tablespoon chili powder
- 1 teaspoon ground cumin
- 1 teaspoon paprika
- ¼ teaspoon cayenne pepper
- ½ pound (1 cup) peeled cooked shrimp
- 2 tablespoons chopped fresh parsley
- 1 teaspoon hot pepper sauce or to taste
- 1 cup rinsed and drained canned light or dark red kidney beans (optional)

Heat a dutch oven (preferably cast iron) over medium-high heat for 1 minute. Place sausage in dutch oven and brown. Using a slotted spoon, transfer sausage to a bowl. Add onion, chile, celery, and garlic to dutch oven and cook for 5 minutes or until onion is translucent. Add thyme and bay leaves and cook for 1 minute more. Add broth and 2 cups of the water and bring to a boil.

Reduce heat, cover tightly, and simmer for 45 minutes. Add ham, tomatoes and their liquid, rice, chili powder, cumin, paprika, cayenne, and remaining 2 cups water. Bring to a boil, reduce heat, cover tightly, and simmer for 20 minutes. Remove dutch oven from heat and stir in shrimp, parsley, hot sauce, and beans (if desired). Cover and let stand for 30 minutes to finish cooking. Flavors improve if chili is refrigerated overnight or for at least 4 hours. Reheat over low heat before serving, sprinkled with additional hot sauce (if desired).

Makes about 8 cups without beans, 9 cups with beans

SUGGESTED GARNISH: Fresh parsley sprigs

Cook's Note: This chili will be heart healthy if turkey kielbasa is substituted.*

Backroad Black-Eyed Pea Chili

Black-eyed peas and mild Italian sausage, simmered slowly with onions, sweet red peppers, and chili powder and served on a bed of white rice, make for a substantial, satisfying chili.

1 tablespoon vegetable oil
1 pound mild Italian sausage, casings removed
2 cups chopped yellow onion
1 cup chopped red bell pepper
5 cups water
2 15-ounce cans black-eyed peas, rinsed and drained
1 bay leaf
½ teaspoon dried thyme leaves
¼ teaspoon cayenne pepper
2 tablespoons chili powder
1 teaspoon ground cumin
1 teaspoon salt
3–4 cups hot cooked white rice
Hot pepper sauce to taste

Place oil in a dutch oven (preferably cast iron) and heat over medium-high heat for 1 minute. Add sausage, brown, and, using a slotted spoon, transfer to paper towels to drain. Pour off excess grease from dutch oven, add onion and red pepper, and cook for 5–6 minutes or until edges of onion are beginning to brown. Add water, peas, bay leaf, thyme, cayenne, and meat. Stir gently but thoroughly, scraping bottom of dutch oven with a flat spatula.

Bring to a boil, reduce heat, and simmer, uncovered, for 20 minutes, stirring occasionally. Remove dutch oven from heat, add chili powder, cumin, and salt, and let stand, uncovered, for 30 minutes. Flavors improve if chili is refrigerated overnight or for at least 4 hours. Reheat over low heat before serving. Spoon over rice and sprinkle with hot pepper sauce.

Makes about 6 cups

SUGGESTED GARNISH: Chopped scallions

Sausage and Shrimp Creole Chili

The mouthwatering down-home gumbo flavor of this chili comes from its distinctive Louisiana-influenced ingredients. Served over hot white rice, it's sure to please anyone longing for a taste of the South.

¾ pound kielbasa sausage, diced (turkey kielbasa may be substituted if desired) (see Note)

2 garlic cloves, minced

1 cup chopped yellow onion

2 fresh Anaheim or New Mexican green chiles, finely chopped, or ½ cup chopped green bell pepper

½ cup chopped celery

1 cup chopped fresh or frozen okra (not canned)

2 14½-ounce cans diced tomatoes, undrained

1 tablespoon fresh lemon juice

2 tablespoons chili powder

1 bay leaf

½ teaspoon dried thyme leaves

¼ teaspoon cayenne pepper

2 cups water

¼ teaspoon salt or to taste

½ pound small shrimp, peeled and deveined (about 1 cup)

3–4 cups hot cooked white rice

Heat a dutch oven (preferably cast iron) over medium-high heat for 1 minute. Add sausage, brown, and, using a slotted spoon, transfer to paper towels to drain. Add garlic, onion, chiles, and celery to any pan drippings and cook for 4 minutes. Add okra, tomatoes and their liquid, lemon juice, chili powder, bay leaf, thyme, cayenne, water, salt, and sausage. Bring to a boil.

Reduce heat and simmer, covered, for 1 hour. Add shrimp, increase heat to high, and return to a boil. Reduce heat and simmer, uncovered, for 10 minutes. Remove dutch oven from heat and let stand, uncovered, for at least 15 minutes before serving. Salt to taste. Flavors improve if chili is refrigerated overnight or for at least 4 hours. Reheat over low heat and serve over rice.

Makes about 5–6 cups

SUGGESTED GARNISH: Cooked peeled shrimp with tails on, lightly tossed in fresh lemon juice and sprinkled with chili powder

Cook's Note: This chili will be heart healthy if turkey kielbasa is substituted.*

Guajillo and Ancho Chili with Ancho-Orange Sauce*

Small pieces of pork and onion are browned and stewed with guajillo and ancho chiles and topped with a delicious, slightly spicy citrus pepper sauce.

Chili

    1 quart plus 2 tablespoons water
    4 dried guajillo chiles
    2 dried ancho chiles
    1 tablespoon vegetable oil
    1 pound boneless lean pork, cut into
        ½-inch pieces
    3 cups chopped yellow onion
    2 garlic cloves, minced
    1 14½-ounce can chicken broth (not
        condensed)
    ¼ teaspoon dried thyme leaves
    1 small bay leaf
    1 tablespoon flour
    ½ teaspoon ground cumin
    1 teaspoon salt or to taste

Ancho-Orange Sauce

    4 dried ancho chiles
    2 cups boiling water
    ½ cup fresh orange juice
    1 tablespoon extra-virgin olive oil

Make the Chili

Bring 2 cups of the water to a boil. Place guajillo and ancho chiles in a medium-size mixing bowl, cover with boiling water, and let stand for 20 minutes to rehydrate.

While chiles are soaking, place 1½ teaspoons of the vegetable oil in a dutch oven (preferably cast iron) and heat over medium-high heat for 1 minute. Add half the pork, brown, and, using a slotted spoon, transfer to a plate. Repeat with remaining oil and pork.

Add onion and garlic to any pan drippings and cook for 5 minutes or until edges of onion begin to brown. Remove dutch oven from heat and set aside.

When chiles are rehydrated, remove from water (discard water). Remove stems, seeds, and membranes from chiles. Wear rubber or plastic gloves while handling chiles. Add chiles to blender with 1 cup of the remaining water. Blend to a smooth paste (about 2 minutes).

Add chile paste to dutch oven and add 1 cup of the remaining water, broth, thyme, bay leaf, pork, and any accumulated juices. Bring to a boil over high heat. Reduce heat, cover tightly, and simmer for 1 hour and 15 minutes.

Combine flour with remaining 2 tablespoons water and mix until smooth. Add to dutch oven with cumin and salt. Stir until well blended and simmer, uncovered, for 10 minutes more or until slightly thickened. Flavors improve and mellow if chili is refrigerated overnight or for at least 4 hours. Reheat over low heat.

MAKE THE SAUCE

Place chiles in a mixing bowl, cover with boiling water, and let stand for 20 minutes to rehydrate. When chiles are rehydrated, remove from water (discard water). Wear rubber or plastic gloves while handling chiles. Remove stems, seeds, and membranes and chop chiles. Whisk together orange juice and olive oil, add to chiles, and let stand for at least 15 minutes to blend flavors. At serving time, spoon mixture over individual bowls of chili and serve immediately.

Makes about 4 cups

Cook's Note: If guajillo chiles are unavailable, dried New Mexican red chiles may be substituted.

Chorizo, Tomato, and Rice Chili

Chorizo, a highly seasoned Mexican sausage, is combined with vegetables, rice, and kidney beans to make an impressively flavorful chili.

7–8 ounces chorizo, removed from casings and diced
1 cup chopped green bell pepper
1 cup chopped yellow onion
½ cup white rice
1 14½-ounce can diced tomatoes, undrained
1 14½-ounce can beef broth (not condensed)
3 cups water
1 15-ounce can dark red kidney beans, rinsed and drained
1 tablespoon chili powder
1 teaspoon ground coriander
1 teaspoon ground cumin
1 tablespoon extra-virgin olive oil

Coat a dutch oven (preferably cast iron) with low-calorie cooking spray and heat over medium-high heat for 1 minute. Add sausage, brown, and, using a slotted spoon, transfer to paper towels to drain. Pour off excess grease from dutch oven, add green pepper and onion, and cook for 4 minutes or until onion is translucent. Add rice and cook for 2 minutes more.

Return meat to dutch oven and add tomatoes and their liquid, broth, water, beans, chili powder, and coriander. Bring to a boil, reduce heat to low, cover tightly, and simmer for 20 minutes. Remove from heat and add cumin and oil. Let stand, uncovered, for 30 minutes before serving. Flavors will blend if chili is refrigerated overnight or for at least 4 hours. Reheat over low heat.

Makes about 6 cups

Suggested garnish: Dark red kidney beans (rinsed and blotted dry with paper towels) tossed with a bit of olive oil and chopped parsley for added flavor and an appetizing sheen. Mound a small amount of beans in the center of each serving.

Country Vegetable and Bacon Chili

Topped with cheddar cheese and roasted pepper strips, this garden vegetable chili makes delicious use of spring and summer produce.

3 green bell peppers
4 slices bacon
1 cup chopped yellow onion
1 cup diced (about 1 medium) yellow
    squash
1/8 cup chopped celery
1 cup shredded green cabbage
1 cup fresh or frozen corn kernels
1 cup fresh or frozen lima beans
2 fresh jalapeño chiles, seeded and
    chopped
2 4-ounce cans green chiles, rinsed and
    drained
1 cup (1 8-ounce can) tomato sauce
2 teaspoons ground cumin
1 teaspoon dried oregano leaves
1 teaspoon salt
1/4 teaspoon black pepper
2 cups water
1 cup (about 1/4 pound) shredded sharp
    cheddar cheese

Preheat broiler. Split green peppers in half lengthwise and remove stems, seeds, and membranes. Flatten peppers with the palm of your hand and place cut-side down on a foil-lined oven rack. Broil 2–3 inches from heat source for 7 minutes or until completely blistered. Transfer to a bowl of ice water for 5 minutes, then peel. Chop two of the peppers, slice remaining pepper into 1/4-inch strips, and set aside.

Heat a dutch oven (preferably cast iron) over medium-high heat for 1 minute. Add bacon and cook until crisp. Transfer to paper towels to drain, then crumble and set aside.

Discard all but 2 tablespoons grease from dutch oven and heat over medium-high heat for about 1 minute. Add onion, squash, and celery and cook for 8–10 minutes or until onion is beginning to brown. Add remaining ingredients except bacon, roasted peppers, and cheese and bring to a boil. Reduce heat, cover tightly, and simmer for 30 minutes.

Add bacon and chopped roasted peppers. Stir to blend thoroughly, top with cheese, and arrange roasted pepper strips decoratively on top. Place under broiler at least 5 inches from heat source for 1–2 minutes or until cheese is completely melted and beginning to bubble, being careful not to burn pepper strips. Let stand, covered, for 10 minutes before serving. Reheat over low heat.

Makes about 8 cups

Chunky Three-Bean and Sausage Chili with Pasta

Spicy chunks of Italian sausage simmered in a beef stock base are complemented here by tomatoes, corn, green chiles, pasta, and garbanzo, black, and kidney beans.

1 pound hot Italian sausage, cut into
1-inch pieces (mild sausage may be
substituted if desired)
1 cup chopped yellow onion
1 cup chopped green bell pepper
2 tablespoons chili powder
1½ teaspoons ground cumin
½ teaspoon dried oregano leaves
1 14½-ounce can diced tomatoes,
undrained
1 14½-ounce can beef broth (not
condensed)
1 cup water
1 cup fresh or frozen corn kernels
1 cup rinsed and drained canned
garbanzo beans
1 cup rinsed and drained
canned black beans

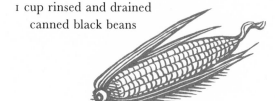

1 cup rinsed and drained canned light or
dark red kidney beans
1 4-ounce can green chiles, rinsed and
drained
2 ounces (½ cup) small pasta shells
½ cup tomato sauce
½ teaspoon sugar
½ teaspoon salt

Heat dutch oven (preferably cast iron) over medium-high heat for 1 minute. Add sausage, brown, and, using a slotted spoon, transfer to paper towels to drain. Pour off excess grease from dutch oven, add onion and green pepper, and cook for 4 minutes or until onion is translucent. Add chili powder, cumin, and oregano and cook for 1 minute more. Add remaining ingredients and bring to a boil. Reduce heat and simmer, covered, for 20 minutes.

Remove from heat. If a thinner consistency is desired, add ½–¾ cup water. Let stand, covered, for 20 minutes before serving. Reheat over low heat. Flavors will be at their peak if chili is then served immediately.

Makes 8–9 cups

Suggested garnish: Crumbled feta cheese

4

Poultry Chilies

Slow-Simmered New Mexican Jalapeño White Bean-Chicken Chili

A mellow, soothing chicken and white bean chili with rich cream, this dish is flavored subtly with fresh garlic and green chiles.

½ pound (about 1 cup) dried Great
    Northern beans
3 quarts water
1 4-pound whole frying chicken
10 garlic cloves, minced
2 cups chopped yellow onion
1 cup chopped green bell pepper
2 4-ounce cans chopped green chiles
1–2 fresh jalapeño chiles, chopped
1 tablespoon chicken bouillon granules
1 tablespoon ground cumin
1 teaspoon ground coriander
1 teaspoon dried oregano leaves
1 tablespoon salt
1 cup half-and-half

Soak beans in 1 quart of the water overnight. Or bring to a boil, boil for 2 minutes, remove from heat, and let stand for 1 hour. Drain well.

In a stockpot, bring remaining 2 quarts water to a boil and add chicken, beans, and garlic. Return to a boil, then reduce heat and simmer, covered, for 1 hour. Remove chicken from pot and set aside.

Add remaining ingredients to stockpot except 1½ teaspoons of the cumin and half-and-half. Increase heat to high and return to a boil. Reduce heat and simmer, uncovered, for 1½ hours. While chili is cooking, as soon as chicken has cooled, remove bones and cut meat into ½-inch pieces. Set aside. When bean mixture has cooked for 1½ hours, remove pot from heat. Place 1 cup of the mixture in a blender and blend until smooth. Return pureed mixture to pot. Blend another cup of bean mixture until smooth. Add half-and-half to puree in blender, process until smooth, and slowly pour into pot. Add chicken and remaining 1½ teaspoons cumin to pot and stir until blended. Let stand, uncovered, for 15 minutes. Reheat over low heat if necessary before serving.

Makes 10–12 cups

Suggested garnish: Small whole green jalapeños

Cook's Note: If chili is to be frozen or made ahead, do not add half-and-half until serving time.

Habanero Chicken Chili

The habanero is one of the hottest chiles in the world. Used sparingly, it provides a manageable fire and a robust flavor. Here it's combined with sweet red peppers, chicken, lime, and rosemary for a deliciously unique chili.

2 tablespoons extra-virgin olive oil
2 cups chopped yellow onion
2 cups chopped red bell pepper
4 garlic cloves, minced
1 quart water
1 dried habanero chile
¾ teaspoon dried rosemary leaves
2 tablespoons fresh lime juice
1 teaspoon ground cumin
1 4-pound frying chicken, cut up
1 tablespoon salt
½ pound medium-size pasta shells, cooked (optional)

Place oil in a dutch oven (preferably cast iron) and heat over medium-high heat for 1 minute. Add onion, red pepper, and garlic and cook for 5–6 minutes or until onion is translucent. Add remaining ingredients except chicken, salt, and pasta. Bring to a boil, add chicken pieces, discarding gizzards and liver, and return to a boil.

Reduce heat and simmer, covered, for 30 minutes. Add salt and simmer, uncovered, for 30 minutes more.

Remove dutch oven from heat, remove chicken, and set aside to cool slightly. Remove bones and cut meat into ½-inch pieces. Bring broth to a boil, and, using a whisk, stir vigorously to break down chile completely. Remove from heat, add chicken, and let stand, uncovered, for 15 minutes before serving. Flavors improve if chili is refrigerated overnight or for at least 4 hours. Reheat over medium heat. Serve by itself or with ½ cup pasta per serving.

Makes about 8 cups

SUGGESTED GARNISH: Paper-thin slices of fresh lime

Cook's Note: Adding the salt during the last half of the cooking process allows the dried chile to rehydrate and begin to break down first. If the salt were added earlier, the chile could not rehydrate properly.

New Mexican Red Chili with Chicken

This simple yet full-flavored dish is served over hot egg noodles.

6 dried New Mexican red chiles
1 quart boiling water
1 tablespoon extra-virgin olive oil
4 (about 1¼ pounds) skinless chicken thighs and 4 (about 1 pound) skinless chicken legs or 4 (2¼ pounds) skinless chicken breast halves (see Note)
2 cups chopped yellow onion
6 garlic cloves, minced
1 14½-ounce can chicken broth (not condensed)
1 teaspoon dried oregano leaves
1 teaspoon salt
½ pound egg noodles, cooked (about 4 cups)

Preheat oven to 250°F. Place dried chiles on a baking sheet and bake for 3 minutes. Place in a bowl, cover with boiling water, and let stand for 15–20 minutes to rehydrate.

While chiles are soaking, place oil in a dutch oven (preferably cast iron) and heat over medium-high heat for 1 minute. Add half of the chicken and brown. Transfer to paper towels to drain and repeat with remaining chicken. Add onion and garlic to any pan drippings and cook for 4 minutes or until onion is translucent. Remove dutch oven from heat and let stand.

Remove chiles from water (reserve water). Remove stems and, for milder chili, seeds and membranes. Wear rubber or plastic gloves while handling chiles. Place chiles in a blender with 1 cup of the chile water and blend until smooth (2–3 minutes). Add to dutch oven with remaining chile water, broth, oregano, and salt. Bring to a boil over high heat, add chicken pieces, and return to a boil. Reduce heat and simmer, uncovered, for 1 hour. Remove from heat and let stand, uncovered, for 45 minutes to thicken and allow flavors to penetrate chicken. Skim off grease. Flavor improves if chili is refrigerated overnight or for at least 4 hours. Reheat chili over moderate heat. Serve over egg noodles.

Makes 4 servings

SUGGESTED GARNISH: Sour cream topped with cilantro leaves

Cook's Note: This chili will be heart healthy if skinless chicken breasts are substituted for the thighs and legs. Cook for only 35–40 minutes.*

Chipotle Chicken Chili

A rich, smoky heat infuses the chicken, creating an outstanding, highly flavored chili. A definite favorite.

    5 cups water
    3 dried chipotle chiles
    2 tablespoons extra-virgin olive oil
    2 pounds (about 7 pieces) skinless chicken
        thighs or skinless chicken breasts (see
        Note)
    2 cups chopped yellow onion
    8 garlic cloves, minced
    2 14½-ounce cans diced tomatoes,
        undrained
    2 teaspoons salt or to taste
    4–5 cups hot cooked white or Spanish-
        seasoned yellow rice

In a small saucepan, bring 1 cup of the water to a boil. Remove from heat, add chipotle chiles, and let stand for 20–30 minutes to rehydrate.

While chiles are soaking, place 1 tablespoon of the oil in a dutch oven (preferably cast iron) and heat over medium-high heat for 1 minute. Add half the chicken, brown, and transfer to a plate. Repeat with remaining chicken. Add onion and garlic to pan drippings and cook for 5–6 minutes or until onion is just beginning to brown. Remove dutch oven from heat.

Remove chiles from water (reserve water). Remove stems, seeds, and membranes and place in a blender with chile water. Wear rubber or plastic gloves while handling chiles. Blend until completely smooth (2–3 minutes). Add to dutch oven with tomatoes and their liquid, chicken and any accumulated juices, and remaining 4 cups water. Bring to a boil over high heat, reduce heat, and simmer, uncovered, for 1 hour. Remove dutch oven from heat.

Remove chicken from pot, remove bones, cut into ½-inch pieces, and return meat to dutch oven with salt. Cook for 10 minutes more. Toss remaining tablespoon of oil with rice and serve chili on rice. Flavors improve if chili is refrigerated overnight or for at least 4 hours. Reheat over low heat before serving.

Makes about 6 cups

Suggested garnish: Sour cream topped with thin slices of black olive, chopped red onion, and cilantro. Crown each serving with a small red or green whole jalapeño.

Cook's Note: This chili will be heart healthy if skinless chicken breasts are substituted for the thighs. Cook for only 35–40 minutes.*

Mild Spanish Chicken and Pepper Chili

Tender peppers and chicken are slow-simmered with bacon and fresh garlic and tossed with olive oil to give this succulent chili a deep, mellow flavor.

4 slices bacon

2 pounds (about 7 pieces) skinless chicken thighs

10 garlic cloves, minced

3 cups chopped green bell pepper

½ teaspoon hot red pepper flakes

5 cups water

1 tablespoon chicken bouillon granules

¼ teaspoon salt

3–4 cups hot cooked white or Spanish-seasoned yellow rice

1 tablespoon extra-virgin olive oil

Heat a dutch oven (preferably cast iron) over medium-high heat for 1 minute. Add bacon and cook until crisp. Drain on paper towels, then crumble and set aside. Discard all but 2 table-spoons grease from dutch oven and add half the chicken. Brown for 5–7 minutes, turning occasionally, then transfer to a plate. Brown the remaining chicken.

Return reserved chicken to dutch oven. Add garlic, green pepper, red pepper flakes, water, bouillon granules, salt, and bacon to dutch oven and bring to a boil. Reduce heat and simmer, uncovered, for 45 minutes. Transfer chicken to a plate and continue to cook vegetables, uncovered, for 15 minutes more. When chicken has cooled slightly, remove bones and cut into ½-inch pieces. Return chicken to pot and cook for 10 minutes more.

Remove dutch oven from heat and let stand, uncovered, for 10 minutes before serving. Flavors are greatly enhanced if chili is refrigerated overnight or for at least 4 hours. At serving time, reheat over low heat and toss rice with olive oil. Spoon chili over rice and serve.

Makes about 5 cups

SUGGESTED GARNISH: Chopped Kalamata olives, finely chopped fresh tomatoes, and chopped parsley

Buffalo Wing Chili

This fiery chili gets its flavor from chicken, tomatoes, and fresh garlic, slow-simmered in Tabasco sauce (with more sauce added just before serving).

2 tablespoons extra-virgin olive oil

2 pounds (about 7 pieces) skinless chicken thighs or skinless chicken breasts (see Note)

2 14½-ounce cans chicken broth (not condensed)

2 14½-ounce cans diced tomatoes, undrained

2 cups water

8 garlic cloves, minced

3 tablespoons Tabasco sauce

Place 1 tablespoon of the oil in a dutch oven (preferably cast iron) and heat over medium-high heat for 1 minute. Add half the chicken, brown, and transfer to a plate. Repeat with remaining chicken.

Return chicken to dutch oven with any accumulated juices and add remaining ingredients except 1 tablespoon Tabasco and remaining olive oil. Bring to a boil, reduce heat, and simmer, uncovered, for 1 hour. Remove dutch oven from heat and remove chicken.

When chicken has cooled slightly, remove bones and cut meat into ½-inch pieces. Bring liquid in dutch oven to a boil, add chicken, remove from heat, and let stand, uncovered, for 15 minutes. Flavors improve if chili is refrigerated overnight or for at least 4 hours. Reheat over low heat. At serving time, stir in remaining Tabasco and oil.

Makes about 5 cups

Suggested garnish: Crumbled blue cheese

Cook's Note: If the chili is to be made ahead, do not add remaining Tabasco and oil until reheated and ready to serve.

This chili will be heart healthy if skinless chicken breasts are substituted for the thighs. Cook for only 35–40 minutes.*

Habanero Calypso Chicken Chili

An exciting, extremely hot combination of chicken, habaneros, fresh ginger, and sweet red peppers, this dish is not for the timid. It's seasoned with citrus and tossed with pineapple for extra flavor.

1–2 dried habanero chiles

1 cup boiling water

1 tablespoon vegetable oil

2 pounds (about 7 pieces) skinless chicken thighs or skinless chicken breasts (see Note)

2 garlic cloves, minced

1 teaspoon grated fresh ginger

½ teaspoon ground allspice

3 cups pineapple-orange juice

1 14½-ounce can chicken broth (not condensed)

2 cups chopped red bell pepper

½ teaspoon ground cumin

1 8-ounce can pineapple tidbits, well drained

Place habanero chile in a bowl, cover with boiling water, and let stand for 20 minutes to rehydrate.

While chile is soaking, place oil in a dutch oven (preferably cast iron) and heat over medium-high heat for 1 minute. Add half the chicken, brown, and transfer to a plate. Repeat with remaining chicken. Add garlic and ginger to any pan drippings and cook for 30 seconds. Add allspice, juice, and broth, remove dutch oven from heat, and set aside.

Remove chile from water (reserve water). Wear rubber or plastic gloves while handling chile. Remove stems, seeds, and membranes and place chile and chile water in a blender. Blend until smooth (2–3 minutes). Add paste to dutch oven, bring to a boil over medium-high heat, scraping bottom and sides of pot, and add chicken pieces and any accumulated juices. Return to a boil, reduce heat, cover tightly, and simmer for 45 minutes.

Remove chicken and set aside to cool slightly. Add bell pepper to dutch oven and cook, uncovered, for 12 minutes. While peppers are cooking, remove bones from chicken and cut meat into ½-inch pieces. Remove dutch oven from heat and add chicken, cumin, and pineapple. Let stand, uncovered, for 10 minutes before serving. Reheat over low heat.

Makes about 4 cups

SUGGESTED GARNISH: Thinly sliced pineapple and fresh mint leaves

Cook's Note: This chili will be heart healthy if skinless chicken breasts are substituted for the thighs. Cook for only 35–40 minutes.*

Cheater's Shredded Chicken Chili

Browned chicken simmered in salsa and chili seasonings, shredded, and served over Spanish rice with scallions gives this dish a slow-cooked flavor without the effort.

- 1 tablespoon extra-virgin olive oil
- 2 pounds (about 7 pieces) skinless chicken thighs
- 1 16-ounce jar thick and chunky extra-mild or mild salsa
- 1 1¾-ounce package chili seasoning mix
- 1 quart water
- 2–3 cups hot cooked white or Spanish-seasoned yellow rice
- 2–3 tablespoons chopped scallion

Place oil in a dutch oven (preferably cast iron) and heat over medium-high heat for 1 minute. Add half the chicken, brown, and transfer to a plate. Repeat with remaining chicken. Pour off excess grease from dutch oven and add salsa, chili seasoning mix, and water. Stir to blend thoroughly, bring to a boil, add chicken and any accumulated juices, and return to a boil. Reduce heat and simmer, uncovered, for 1 hour.

Remove dutch oven from heat and remove chicken. When cooled slightly, remove bones and shred meat with a fork. Return chicken to pot and heat over medium heat for 5 minutes. Flavors improve if chili is refrigerated overnight or for at least 4 hours. Reheat over medium heat. Serve over rice tossed with chopped scallion.

Makes about 4 cups

SUGGESTED GARNISH: Sour cream

Pepper Chicken Chili*

This is a colorful, vividly flavored blend of fresh, roasted, and dried peppers, sun-dried tomatoes, onions, and chicken.

- 4 dried New Mexican red chiles
- 1 dried ancho chile
- 8 sun-dried tomatoes
- 3 cups boiling water
- 4 fresh New Mexican or Anaheim green chiles
- 3 tablespoons extra-virgin olive oil
- 2 garlic cloves, minced
- 1 red bell pepper, chopped
- 1 yellow bell pepper, chopped
- 1 orange bell pepper, chopped
- 1 green bell pepper, chopped

1 cup chopped yellow onion

4 scallions, chopped

1 pound skinless, boneless chicken breasts, cut into ½-inch pieces

½ teaspoon dried basil leaves

1 cup chopped fresh parsley

3 cups canned chicken broth (not condensed)

1 tablespoon fresh lime juice

Salt to taste

2–3 cups hot cooked white or Spanish-seasoned yellow rice, no salt or oil added during cooking

Preheat broiler. Place dried chiles and tomatoes in a bowl, cover with boiling water, and let stand for 3 minutes. Remove tomatoes, chop, and set aside. Let chiles stand for 20 minutes longer to rehydrate.

While dried chiles are soaking, place green chiles on a foil-lined oven rack and broil 2–3 inches from heat source for 10–12 minutes or until completely blistered, turning ccasionally.

Transfer to a bowl of ice water and let stand for 5 minutes. Peel, and remove stems, seeds, and membranes, chop, and set aside.

Remove chiles from water (reserving ½ cup water). Remove stems, seeds, and membranes and place chiles in a blender with chile water. Wear rubber or plastic gloves while handling chiles. Blend to a smooth paste (about 2–3 minutes).

Place oil in a dutch oven (preferably cast iron) and heat over medium-high heat for 2 minutes. Add garlic, bell peppers, onion, scallion, chicken, basil, chopped green chiles, sun-dried tomatoes, chile paste, and parsley. Cook for 5 minutes, add broth, and cook, uncovered, for 10 minutes. Remove dutch oven from heat, add lime juice, stir to blend, and let stand, uncovered, for 15 minutes before serving. Reheat over low heat if necessary. Add salt and serve over rice.

Makes about 4 cups

SUGGESTED GARNISH: Thin rings of orange, yellow, and red bell pepper

Salsa Verde Chicken Chili

This chicken chili is seasoned with smoked jalapeño chile, onion, and tomatillo salsa.

- 1 dried chipotle chile
- 1 cup boiling water
- 1 tablespoon extra-virgin olive oil
- 2 pounds (about 7 pieces) skinless chicken thighs
- 2 cups chopped yellow onion
- ½ teaspoon dried oregano
- 1 16-ounce bottle mild salsa verde (with tomatillos if possible)
- 2 14½-ounce cans reduced-sodium chicken broth

Place chile in a bowl, cover with boiling water, and let stand for 30 minutes to rehydrate. While chile is soaking, place oil in a dutch oven (preferably cast iron) and heat over medium-high heat for 1 minute. Add half the chicken, brown, and transfer to a plate. Repeat with remaining chicken. Add onion to any pan drippings and cook for 4 minutes or until onion is translucent. Remove dutch oven from heat and set aside.

Remove chile from water (reserve water). Remove stems, seeds, and membranes from chile and place in a blender with chile water. Wear rubber or plastic gloves while handling chile. Blend until smooth (about 2 minutes). Add to dutch oven and stir, scraping bottom and sides. Add oregano, salsa, and broth and bring to a boil. Add chicken and return to a boil. Reduce heat and simmer, uncovered, for 45 minutes. Remove dutch oven from heat and remove chicken. When cooled slightly, remove bones and shred meat with a fork. Return to pot, cover, and let stand for 5 minutes. Flavors improve if chili is refrigerated overnight or for at least 4 hours. Reheat over low heat before serving.

Makes about 4 cups

SUGGESTED GARNISH: Grated Monterey Jack cheese

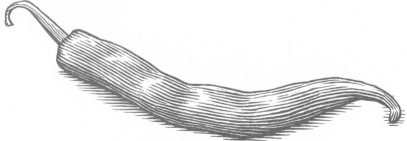

Lean Mean Game-Time Chili*

This flavor-packed, guilt-free chili is made with heart-healthy turkey sausage, fresh garlic, and other seasonings and is crowned with generous dollops of nonfat sour cream, red onion, and cilantro.

2 12-ounce packages turkey bulk sausage
1 pound lean ground turkey
2 cups chopped yellow onion
1 cup chopped green bell pepper
6 garlic cloves, minced
¼ cup chili powder
2 tablespoons ground cumin
1½ teaspoons ground coriander
1 teaspoon sugar
½ teaspoon hot red pepper flakes
2 14½-ounce cans diced tomatoes, undrained
1 14½-ounce can beef broth (not condensed)
¼ cup tomato paste
2 15-ounce cans dark red kidney beans, rinsed and drained
Nonfat sour cream
Finely chopped red onion
Chopped fresh cilantro leaves

Coat a dutch oven (preferably cast iron) with low-calorie cooking spray and heat over medium-high heat for 1 minute. Add half the meat and brown, crumbling with a fork. Using a slotted spoon, transfer to paper towels to drain. Repeat with remaining meat. Dry dutch oven with paper towels and recoat with cooking spray. Add onion, green pepper, and garlic and cook for 5–6 minutes or until edges of onion are beginning to brown.

Add chili powder, 1 tablespoon of the cumin, coriander, sugar, hot red pepper flakes, tomatoes and their liquid, broth, tomato paste, and beans. Stir in meat, bring to a boil, reduce heat to low, and simmer, uncovered, for 30 minutes. Stir in remaining tablespoon of cumin and let stand, uncovered, for 15 minutes. Flavors improve if chili is refrigerated overnight or for at least 4 hours. Reheat over low heat before serving with dollops of sour cream and topped with red onion and cilantro.

Makes about 10 cups

Hot Roasted Jalapeño and Turkey Chili*

This light chili combines turkey, roasted peppers, tomatoes, and jalapeños. Seasoned with olive oil and served over hot rice, it's a wonderful choice for cool summer evenings.

2 green bell peppers
2 tablespoons extra-virgin olive oil
1 pound turkey tenderloins, cut into
    ½-inch pieces
4 fresh jalapeño chiles, seeded and
    chopped
4 cloves garlic, minced
2 14½-ounce cans chicken broth (not
    condensed)
1 14½-ounce can diced tomatoes,
    undrained
1 tablespoon chili powder
½ teaspoon paprika
1 teaspoon ground cumin
1 teaspoon hot pepper sauce
3–4 cups hot cooked white or Spanish-
    seasoned yellow rice, no salt or oil
    added during cooking

Preheat broiler. Cut green peppers in half lengthwise, place cut-side down on a foil-lined oven rack, and flatten with the palm of your hand. Broil 2–3 inches from heat source for 7 minutes or until completely blistered. Transfer to a bowl of ice water and set aside for 5 minutes. Peel, chop, and set aside.

Place 1 tablespoon of the oil in a dutch oven (preferably cast iron) and heat over medium heat for 1 minute. Add turkey and cook until no longer pink. Add jalapeños, garlic, broth, tomatoes and their liquid, chili powder, paprika, cumin, and chopped peppers. Bring to a boil, reduce heat, and simmer, uncovered, for 15 minutes. Remove dutch oven from heat, stir in remaining tablespoon of oil and hot pepper sauce, and let stand, uncovered, for 15 minutes. Flavors improve if chili is refrigerated overnight or for at least 4 hours. Reheat over medium heat before serving over rice.

Makes about 6 cups

SUGGESTED GARNISH: Sour cream, minced fresh jalapeño, and lime wedges

Mediterranean Chili*

A savory blend of sausage, beans, eggplant, zucchini, yellow squash, and cheese gives this dish a mouthwatering variety of colors and flavors.

½ pound turkey bulk sausage
¾ cup chopped yellow onion
½ cup chopped green bell pepper
2 garlic cloves, minced
1½ teaspoons chili powder
¼ teaspoon dried oregano leaves
¼ teaspoon hot red pepper flakes
¼ teaspoon fennel seeds
1 cup peeled and diced eggplant
½ cup diced zucchini
½ cup diced yellow squash
1 14½-ounce can diced tomatoes, drained
2 tablespoons chopped fresh parsley
1 tablespoon dry red wine
2 teaspoons beef bouillon granules
1 quart water
1 15-ounce can dark red kidney beans, rinsed and drained
1 tablespoon extra-virgin olive oil
1 cup (¼ pound) grated mozzarella cheese
2 tablespoons freshly grated Parmesan cheese

Coat a dutch oven (preferably cast iron) with low-calorie cooking spray and heat over medium-high heat for 1 minute. Add sausage and brown, crumbling with a fork. Add onion, green pepper, garlic, chili powder, oregano, red pepper flakes, and fennel. Cook for 4 minutes or until onion is translucent. Add eggplant, zucchini, yellow squash, tomatoes, parsley, wine, bouillon granules, and water.

Bring to a boil, reduce heat, and simmer, uncovered, for 1 hour. Add beans and cook for 5 minutes more. Remove dutch oven from heat, stir in oil, and let stand, uncovered, for 15 minutes before serving. Flavors improve if chili is refrigerated overnight or for at least 4 hours. Reheat over medium heat. Top each serving with about 2½ tablespoons mozzarella and 1 teaspoon Parmesan cheese.

Makes about 6 cups

SUGGESTED GARNISH: Fresh parsley sprigs

Indian Summer Spiced Turkey Chili with Wild Rice and Toasted Pecans

Sausage, wild rice, butternut squash, and dark red kidney beans are seasoned with savory spices and topped with toasted pecans.

1 12-ounce package turkey bulk sausage
¼ cup wild rice
¼ cup brown rice
1 cup chopped yellow onion
½ cup finely chopped red bell pepper
2 teaspoons allspice
1 teaspoon paprika
1 teaspoon ground cinnamon
1 teaspoon ground cumin
¼ teaspoon ground nutmeg
½ teaspoon hot red pepper flakes
¼ teaspoon cayenne pepper
2 teaspoons dark brown sugar
6 cups water
2 cups butternut squash, cut into ½-inch pieces (optional)
1 15-ounce can dark red kidney beans, rinsed and drained
¼ teaspoon salt
1 cup pecan pieces, toasted in broiler (see Note)

Coat a dutch oven (preferably cast iron) with low-calorie cooking spray and heat over medium-high heat for 1 minute. Add sausage and brown, crumbling with a fork. Add wild and brown rice, onion, red pepper, allspice, paprika, cinnamon, cumin, nutmeg, red pepper flakes, cayenne, and brown sugar and cook for 2 minutes.

Add water, bring to a boil, reduce heat, cover tightly, and simmer for 40 minutes. Add squash (if desired), beans, and salt. Cover tightly and cook for 20 minutes more. Remove dutch oven from heat and add ½–¾ cup hot water. Let stand for 20–30 minutes to absorb flavors. Flavors will be at their peak if chili is served after 30 minutes. Reheat over low heat. At serving time, top with toasted pecan pieces.

Makes about 6 cups

SUGGESTED GARNISH: Thinly sliced red bell pepper strips

Cook's Note: To toast pecans in broiler, preheat broiler. Place the pecan pieces in a broiling pan and broil 5 inches from heat source for 30 seconds to 1 minute or until they begin to brown. Be careful not to burn them.

Lentil Turkey Sausage Chili with Cinnamon*

Uniquely flavored, this Morocco-inspired chili combines tender lentils, sausage, and a delicate seasoning of cinnamon and cumin.

6 cups water
½ pound dried lentils, rinsed
1 12-ounce package turkey bulk sausage
1½ cups chopped yellow onion
4 garlic cloves, minced
1 tablespoon chili powder
1 teaspoon ground cinnamon
2 teaspoons ground cumin
1 tablespoon beef bouillon granules
1 teaspoon paprika
¼ teaspoon black pepper
2 tablespoons ketchup

In a small saucepan, bring 2 cups of the water to a boil over high heat, add lentils, and return to a boil. Reduce heat and simmer, uncovered, for 10 minutes. Drain and set aside.

While lentils are cooling, coat a dutch oven (preferably cast iron) with low-calorie cooking spray and heat over medium-high heat for 1 minute. Add sausage and brown, crumbling with a fork. Using a slotted spoon, transfer to paper towels to drain. Add onion, garlic, chili powder, cinnamon, and 1 teaspoon of the cumin to any pan drippings and cook for 5–6 minutes or until edges of onion begin to brown.

Add bouillon granules, paprika, pepper, ketchup, and remaining quart of water to dutch oven. Bring to a boil, add lentils and sausage, return to a boil, reduce heat, and simmer, uncovered, for 25 minutes. Remove from heat, stir in remaining teaspoon of cumin, and let stand, uncovered, for 15 minutes before serving. Reheat over low heat if necessary before serving.

Makes about 6 cups

SUGGESTED GARNISH: Finely chopped scallions

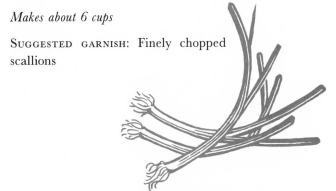

Harvest Chili with Wild Rice

This rustic chili of sausage, wild rice, sweet red peppers, kidney beans, and yellow corn makes a wonderful meal on blustery fall days.

1 12-ounce package turkey bulk sausage
4 garlic cloves, minced
2 tablespoons chili powder
1 6-ounce box long grain and wild rice
    with seasoning packet
1½ cups chopped scallion
1 cup chopped red bell pepper
½ cup chopped celery
1 15-ounce can dark red kidney beans,
    rinsed and drained
2 quarts water
1 tablespoon Worcestershire sauce
1 cup fresh or frozen corn kernels
½ teaspoon salt
1 teaspoon ground cumin

Coat a dutch oven (preferably cast iron) with low-calorie cooking spray and heat over medium-high heat for 1 minute. Add sausage, garlic, and chili powder, and brown, crumbling with a fork. Add rice, seasoning packet, scallion, red pepper, celery, beans, water, and Worcestershire sauce. Bring to a boil, reduce heat, and simmer, covered, for 18 minutes.

Remove dutch oven from heat, stir in corn, salt, and cumin, cover, and let stand for 10 minutes before serving. For a thicker consistency and for peak flavor, let stand for 30 minutes. Reheat over low heat before serving.

Makes 8–10 cups

SUGGESTED GARNISH:
Finely chopped red
bell pepper and
scallions

5

Vegetable Chilies

Yucatecan Black Bean, Lime, and Cilantro Chili*

This fairly thick black bean chili is flavored with fresh garlic, lime, cilantro leaves, seasonings, and olive oil.

- 2 tablespoons extra-virgin olive oil
- 8 garlic cloves, minced
- 1 cup chopped yellow onion
- 1 tablespoon chili powder
- 1½ teaspoons ground cumin
- ¼ teaspoon black pepper
- 2 15-ounce cans black beans, rinsed and drained
- 3 14½-ounce cans reduced-sodium chicken broth (not condensed)
- 2 tablespoons fresh lime juice
- ½ cup chopped fresh cilantro leaves
- ¼ cup chopped radishes
- 1 lime cut into 8 wedges

Place 1 tablespoon of the oil in a dutch oven (preferably cast iron) and heat over medium-high heat for 1 minute. Add garlic and onion and cook for 4 minutes or until onion is translucent. Add chili powder, ½ teaspoon of the cumin, and black pepper and cook for 1 minute. Add beans, broth, and lime juice and bring to a boil. Reduce heat and simmer, uncovered, for 15 minutes.

Transfer 1 cup of the bean mixture to a blender and blend until smooth. Return puree to dutch oven and add ¼ cup of the cilantro and remaining teaspoon of cumin. Simmer, uncovered, for 10 minutes more. Remove from heat, stir in remaining tablespoon of oil, and let stand, uncovered, for 30 minutes to thicken slightly. Reheat over low heat.

At serving time, top with remaining cilantro and radishes and serve with lime wedges.

Makes about 5–6 cups

Cook's Note: Cooking the chili powder and cumin before adding liquid toasts the seasonings and makes their flavors more distinctive.

Mild Black Bean and Rice Chili with Hot Jalapeño-Lime Oil*

This is one of my favorite recipes—lightly seasoned black bean chili served over white rice and topped with a tantalizing blend of jalapeños and serranos, olive oil, fresh lime juice, and garlic.

CHILI

2 tablespoons extra-virgin olive oil

1 cup finely chopped yellow onion

2 fresh Anaheim or New Mexican green chiles, finely chopped (½ cup chopped green bell pepper may be substituted if desired)

3 garlic cloves, minced

2 15-ounce cans black beans, rinsed and drained

3 cups canned chicken broth (not condensed)

2 tablespoons fresh lime juice

2 cups hot cooked white rice, no salt or oil added during cooking

JALAPEÑO-LIME OIL

1 cup extra-virgin olive oil

6 tablespoons fresh lime juice

8 fresh jalapeño chiles, seeded and chopped

4 fresh serrano chiles, seeded and chopped

½ teaspoon salt

½ teaspoon black pepper

4 garlic cloves, minced

MAKE THE CHILI

Place oil in a dutch oven and heat over medium heat for 1 minute. Add onion, chiles, and garlic and cook for 4 minutes or until onion is translucent, stirring frequently. Increase heat to medium-high, add beans, and cook for 2 minutes, stirring gently. Add broth and lime juice. Stir gently to blend, bring to a boil, reduce heat, and simmer, uncovered, for 30 minutes. Meanwhile, prepare oil.

MAKE THE OIL

Place all the ingredients in a small saucepan and whisk together. Bring just to a boil, reduce heat, and simmer for 10 minutes, stirring frequently and skimming off any foam.

At serving time, reheat sauce. Spoon about ½ cup rice into each bowl and place 1 cup chili on top. Pass sauce at the table or spoon about 1–2 tablespoons onto each serving.

Makes about 4 cups chili, about 1 cup oil

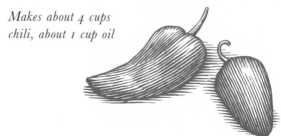

SUGGESTED GARNISH: Thin slices of fresh serrano chile and lime wedges

Cook's Note: You may refrigerate any remaining oil for up to 10 days.

East Indian Hot Pepper–Lentil Chili with Fresh Ginger*

Complex Eastern flavors of hot chiles, fresh ginger, cilantro leaves, and lime infuse this chili with a hint of sweetness and a touch of peppery fire.

- 3 cups water
- 2 10-ounce cans condensed chicken broth
- 2 cups dried lentils, rinsed
- 1/4 teaspoon ground turmeric
- 6 whole dried chiles de árbol or
  - 1/2–1 teaspoon hot red pepper flakes
- 2 tablespoons vegetable oil
- 1 cup chopped yellow onion
- 1/4 cup finely chopped carrot
- 2 tablespoons grated fresh ginger
- 1 teaspoon curry powder
- 1 plum tomato, seeded and chopped
- 1 cup chopped fresh cilantro leaves
- 3 tablespoons fresh lime juice
- 1 1/4 teaspoons sugar
- 1 teaspoon ground cumin

Place water and broth in a dutch oven (preferably cast iron) and bring to a boil over high heat. Add lentils, turmeric, and one of the dried chiles (or all of the red pepper flakes) and return to a boil. Reduce heat, cover tightly, and simmer for 20 minutes.

While lentils are cooking, place oil in a 12-inch nonstick skillet and heat over medium-high heat for 1 minute. Add remaining dried chiles, onion, carrot, ginger, and curry and cook for 8 minutes or until edges of onion just begin to brown. Transfer onion mixture to dutch oven with lentils and add tomato and cilantro. Cook for 5 minutes or until lentils are tender. Remove from heat and stir in lime juice, sugar, and cumin. Let stand, uncovered, for 10–15 minutes to thicken. Reheat over low heat before serving.

Makes 6 cups

SUGGESTED GARNISH: Sprigs of cilantro leaves

Sofrito Black Bean Rice Chili

Sofrito is a delicious, mildly seasoned paste of tomatoes, peppers, onions, garlic, and herbs, pureed and cooked in olive oil. Here it's added to beans and rice for a hearty, nutrition-packed chili.

4 plum tomatoes
1 medium-size green bell pepper, coarsely chopped
1 medium-size yellow onion, coarsely chopped
2 garlic cloves, peeled
¼ cup chopped fresh parsley
½ cup chopped fresh cilantro leaves
2 fresh serrano chiles, stems removed
1 teaspoon dried oregano leaves
1 teaspoon ground cumin
¼ cup extra-virgin olive oil
1 6-ounce can tomato paste

6¼ cups water
2 15-ounce cans black beans, rinsed and drained
1½ teaspoons salt or to taste (see Note)
1 cup converted rice
½ cup sliced pimiento-stuffed green olives
2 teaspoons drained capers
Feta cheese, crumbled (optional) (see Note)

In a blender (*not* a food processor), combine tomatoes, bell pepper, onion, garlic, parsley, ¼ cup of the cilantro, serranos, oregano, and cumin to make the sofrito. Blend to a soupy paste consistency.

Place 2 tablespoons of the oil in a dutch oven (preferably cast iron) and heat over medium heat for 2 minutes. Add the sofrito and cook for 30 minutes, stirring frequently, or until a thick paste is formed. Remove dutch oven from heat and transfer half the sofrito to a bowl.

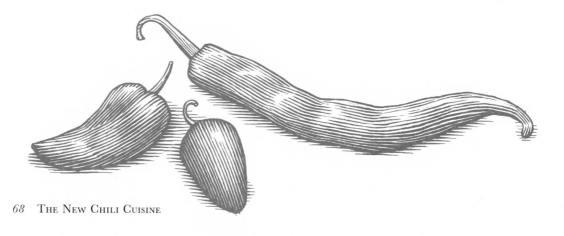

Add half the tomato paste and 1 quart of the water to the sofrito left in the dutch oven and whisk until smooth. Add beans and ½ teaspoon of the salt and stir to blend. Bring to a boil over high heat, reduce heat, and simmer, uncovered, for 20 minutes. Remove dutch oven from heat, add 1 tablespoon of the remaining oil, and let stand for 10–15 minutes to thicken slightly.

While the chili is standing, place rice in a 10-inch skillet (preferably cast iron) over medium-high heat and cook for 4 minutes, stirring constantly. Immediately transfer rice to a plate to stop cooking. Add remaining 2¼ cups water to skillet, bring to a boil, and whisk in remaining sofrito, tomato paste, and salt. Add rice, return liquid to a boil, reduce heat to low, cover tightly, and simmer for 20 minutes. Remove from heat and let stand for 10 minutes. Stir in remaining tablespoon of oil, olives, and capers. Spoon chili into individual bowls, top with rice mixture, and sprinkle with remaining cilantro and crumbled feta (if desired). Flavors will be at their peak if chili is served immediately.

Makes about 4 cups chili, about 4 cups rice

Cook's Note: This chili will be heart healthy if you use only 1 teaspoon salt or less and omit the feta cheese.*

Burgundy Black Bean Chili with Cayenne Cream

Black beans, onions, jalapeños, and seasonings are simmered here in a red wine–beef broth and topped with a refreshing blend of sour cream, olive oil, lime juice, and cayenne pepper.

CHILI

2 tablespoons extra-virgin olive oil
2 cups finely chopped yellow onion
1 medium-size green bell pepper, chopped
2 garlic cloves, minced
2 tablespoons dry red wine
1½ teaspoons chili powder
½ teaspoon dried oregano leaves
1 bay leaf
2 15-ounce cans black beans, rinsed and drained
3 14½-ounce cans beef broth (not condensed)
4 jalapeño chiles, seeded and chopped
½ teaspoon ground cumin
3 cups hot cooked rice

CAYENNE CREAM

1 cup nonfat sour cream
3 tablespoons extra-virgin olive oil
1 tablespoon plus 1 teaspoon fresh lime juice

½ teaspoon salt (see Note)
½ teaspoon cayenne pepper

Place oil in a dutch oven (preferably cast iron) and heat over medium-high heat for 1 minute. Add onion, green pepper, and garlic and cook for 5 minutes or until onion is translucent. Add wine, chili powder, oregano, bay leaf, beans, broth, and jalapeños. Bring to a boil, reduce heat, and simmer, uncovered, for 40 minutes.

Transfer 1 cup of the bean mixture to a blender and process until smooth. Return puree to dutch oven, add cumin, and simmer for 10 minutes more. Remove from heat and let stand, uncovered, for 15 minutes to thicken slightly. Flavors improve if chili is refrigerated overnight or for at least 4 hours.

While chili is standing, combine ingredients for cayenne cream and refrigerate for up to 30 minutes.

At serving time, reheat chili over low heat. Place ½ cup cooked rice in each bowl, top with 1 cup of the chili, and top with a dollop of cream.

Makes 5–6 cups chili, about 1 cup cream

SUGGESTED GARNISH: Lime wedges

Cook's Note: This chili will be heart healthy if the salt in the Cayenne Cream is omitted.*

Ratatouille Chili with Fresh Parmesan*

Fresh mushrooms, eggplant, pole beans, zucchini, and dark red kidney beans are simmered in herbs and tomato sauce, spooned over rotini pasta, and topped with olive oil and fresh Parmesan cheese.

2 tablespoons extra-virgin olive oil
2 cups quartered mushrooms
2 cups diced eggplant
1 cup chopped yellow onion
1 cup chopped green bell pepper
2 garlic cloves, minced
1 cup chopped zucchini
1 cup fresh pole beans, cut into 1-inch
    pieces
1 14½-ounce can diced tomatoes,
    undrained
1 cup canned reduced-sodium chicken
    broth or water (not condensed)
1 8-ounce can tomato sauce
1 tablespoon chili powder
½ teaspoon dried basil leaves
¼ teaspoon hot red pepper flakes
2 tablespoons chopped
    fresh parsley

1 15-ounce can dark red kidney beans,
    rinsed and drained
½ teaspoon salt
¼ cup freshly grated Parmesan cheese
3 cups hot cooked rotini pasta, no salt or
    oil added during cooking (optional)

Place 1 tablespoon of the oil in a dutch oven (preferably cast iron) and heat over medium-high heat for 1 minute. Add mushrooms, eggplant, onion, pepper, and garlic and cook for 10–12 minutes or until onion is translucent. Add zucchini, pole beans, tomatoes and their liquid, chicken broth, tomato sauce, chili powder, basil, red pepper flakes, and parsley. Bring to a boil, reduce heat, cover tightly, and simmer for 20 minutes.

Remove from heat, stir in kidney beans and salt, and blend well. Gently stir in remaining tablespoon of oil and let stand, uncovered, for 15 minutes before serving. Flavors improve if chili is refrigerated overnight or for at least 4 hours. Reheat over low heat. Serve over cooked rotini (if desired) and top with Parmesan.

Makes about 6 cups

SUGGESTED GARNISH: Fresh parsley sprigs

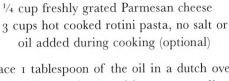

Lentil Chili with Fresh Garden Salsa

Lentils, onions, and peppers are seasoned with soy, fresh ginger, hot chiles, and cumin and served with a crisp, clean-tasting Indonesian salsa.

CHILI

6 cups water

1 cup dried lentils, rinsed

2 tablespoons vegetable oil

1 cup slivered yellow onion

1 cup slivered green bell pepper

2 garlic cloves, minced

½ teaspoon grated fresh ginger

¼–½ teaspoon hot red pepper flakes, to taste

2 14½-ounce cans reduced-sodium chicken broth (not condensed)

¼ cup reduced-sodium soy sauce

1½ teaspoons chili powder

½ teaspoon ground cumin

2–3 cups hot cooked white rice

¼ cup chopped scallion

SALSA

1½ cups peeled, seeded, and finely chopped cucumber

½ cup finely chopped red onion

⅓ cup finely chopped radish

1½ tablespoons grated fresh ginger

1 teaspoon minced garlic

1½ tablespoons fresh lime juice

1 tablespoon sugar

¼ teaspoon hot red pepper flakes

Make the Chili

Place water in a dutch oven (preferably cast iron) and bring to a boil over high heat. Add lentils, return to a boil, reduce heat, and simmer, uncovered, for 20 minutes.

While lentils are cooking, place oil in a 10-inch skillet and heat over medium-high heat for 2 minutes. Add onion, green pepper, garlic, ginger, and red pepper flakes and cook for 4 minutes or until onion is translucent. Add broth and 2 tablespoons of the soy sauce, bring to a boil, reduce heat to low, and simmer, uncovered, for 15 minutes.

Drain lentils and add to vegetable mixture in skillet along with chili powder and cumin. Cook for 5 minutes more or until lentils are just tender. Remove from heat and let stand, uncovered, for 15 minutes before serving. Serve over rice, sprinkle with remaining soy sauce, and top with scallion or salsa.

Make the Salsa

In a small nonmetallic bowl, combine all ingredients. Refrigerate for at least 30 minutes before serving.

Makes about 4 cups chili, about 2 cups salsa

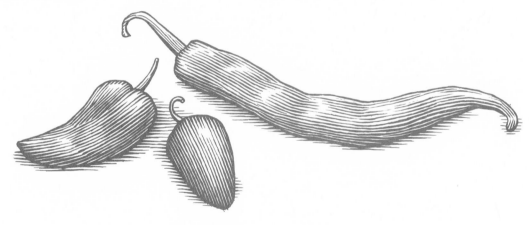

Vegetable Mélange Chili with Jalapeño-Lime Sour Cream*

This tomato-based chili is packed with flavorful, nutritious vegetables.

CHILI

- 1 tablespoon extra-virgin olive oil
- 2 garlic cloves, minced
- 1 cup chopped green bell pepper
- 1 cup chopped yellow onion
- 1 cup sliced mushrooms
- 1 cup small cauliflower florets
- 1 cup diced or sliced carrot
- 1 cup fresh or frozen green beans in 1-inch pieces
- 1 small zucchini, sliced thin
- 1/2 28-ounce can tomatoes packed in puree
- 1 8-ounce can tomato sauce
- 1 15-ounce can dark red kidney beans, rinsed and drained
- 2 cups water or canned beef broth (not condensed)
- 2 tablespoons chili powder
- 1 1/2 teaspoons ground cumin
- 1 teaspoon dried oregano leaves

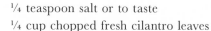

- 1/4 teaspoon salt or to taste
- 1/4 cup chopped fresh cilantro leaves

JALAPEÑO-LIME SOUR CREAM

- 1 1/4 cups nonfat sour cream
- 4 fresh jalapeño chiles, stemmed, halved, and seeded (for less heat)
- 2 tablespoons fresh lime juice
- 2 tablespoons extra-virgin olive oil
- 1/2–3/4 teaspoon salt, to taste

MAKE THE CHILI

Place oil in a dutch oven (preferably cast iron) and heat over medium-high heat for 1 minute. Add garlic, green pepper, and onion and cook for 6 minutes or until onion is translucent. Add remaining ingredients except cilantro (omit salt if using beef broth) and bring to a boil. Reduce heat to low, cover tightly, and simmer for 30 minutes. Remove from heat and let stand for at least 15 minutes before serving. Flavors improve greatly if chili is refrigerated overnight or for at least 4 hours. Reheat over low heat before serving.

MAKE THE SAUCE

No more than in hour before serving, place all ingredients except 1/4 cup of the sour cream in a blender and blend until smooth. Transfer to a bowl, add remaining 1/4 cup sour cream, and whisk until smooth. Refrigerate for 30 minutes to thicken slightly.

At serving time, stir cilantro into chili and top each serving with 1–2 tablespoons cream.

Makes 7–8 cups chili, about 1⅓ cups cream

East Indian Chili with Saffron Rice, Dates, and Toasted Cashews*

In this exotic dish, kidney beans are combined with a curry of cumin, coriander, cardamom, and cloves and topped with saffron rice and dates, toasted cashews, and chopped scallion.

2 tablespoons vegetable oil
½ cup finely chopped yellow onion
1 8-ounce can tomato sauce
2 15-ounce cans light red kidney beans, rinsed and drained
1 quart water
1 teaspoon ground cumin
1 teaspoon ground coriander
½ teaspoon ground ginger
⅛ teaspoon ground cloves
¼ teaspoon cayenne pepper
¼ teaspoon ground cardamom
1 5-ounce package yellow saffron rice, no salt or oil added

¼ cup chopped dates or dried apricots
¼ cup cashew halves, toasted (see Note)
2–3 tablespoons finely chopped scallion

Place 1 tablespoon of the oil in a dutch oven (preferably cast iron) and heat over medium heat for 1 minute. Add onion and cook for 3 minutes or until soft. Add tomato sauce, beans, and water. Bring to a boil, reduce heat, and simmer, uncovered, for 10 minutes.

While bean mixture is simmering, place remaining tablespoon of oil in a small skillet over medium heat and add cumin, coriander, ginger, cloves, cayenne, and cardamom. Cook for about 1 minute or until aromatic. Add spices to beans, stir to blend, and simmer for 15 minutes more. Remove from heat and let stand, uncovered, for 15 minutes. Reheat over low heat before serving.

While chili is standing, cook rice according to package directions. Toss cooked rice with dates, cashews, and scallion. Spoon chili into bowls, spoon rice on top, and serve immediately.

Makes about 4 cups

Suggested garnish: Toasted cashew pieces

Cook's Note: To toast the cashews, preheat broiler. Place cashews in broiler pan and broil 5 inches from heat source for 30 seconds or until cashews are just beginning to brown.

Hot Curry Habanero Chili Topped with Cooling Citrus*

This dish is a delicious example of how eclectic chili can be.

- 2½ cups water
- 1 dried habanero chile
- 2 tablespoons vegetable oil
- 2 cups chopped yellow onion
- 1 cup chopped red bell pepper
- 2 15-ounce cans black beans, rinsed and drained
- 1 garlic clove, minced
- 1 teaspoon grated fresh ginger
- 2 teaspoons curry powder
- 1 cup chopped scallion
- ½ teaspoon salt
- ¼ cup tomato paste
- ½ cup fresh orange juice
- 3 cups hot cooked yellow saffron rice, no salt or oil added during cooking

Bring 1 cup of the water to a boil in a small saucepan, add chile, reduce heat, cover tightly, and simmer for 8–10 minutes to rehydrate chile. Remove pan from heat and remove chile from water (reserve water). Remove stems, seeds, and membranes and place chile in a blender with another cup of cold water.

Wear rubber or plastic gloves while handling chile. Blend until smooth (2–3 minutes). Set aside.

Place oil in a dutch oven (preferably cast iron) and heat over medium-high heat for 1 minute. Add onion and cook for 8–10 minutes or until richly browned. Add red pepper, beans, garlic, ginger, and curry and cook for 2 minutes more. Add chile paste, reserved chile water, ¾ cup of the scallion, and salt. Bring just to a boil, reduce heat, and simmer, uncovered, for 20 minutes.

In a small bowl, combine remaining ½ cup water with tomato paste and whisk until smooth. Add to chili and simmer for 5 minutes. Remove dutch oven from heat and stir in orange juice. Serve immediately for peak flavor. If a thinner consistency is desired, add equal amounts of orange juice and water until desired consistency is achieved. Place chili in individual bowls and spoon rice on top.

Makes about 5 cups

Suggested garnish: Navel orange slices and sliced scallions

6

Quick and Easy Chilies

Beef Chilies

▼▼▼

Piccadillo Beef Chili with Toasted Almond Rice

Ground beef is simmered with onions, serrano chiles, tomatoes, and sweet spices. Tossed with raisins and served with hot rice and richly toasted slivered almonds, this chili combines intriguing flavors and quick-cook appeal.

1 pound ground chuck
1 cup chopped yellow onion
2 garlic cloves, minced
1 fresh serrano chile, seeded and chopped
1 14½-ounce can diced tomatoes, drained
½ teaspoon salt
1 bay leaf
¼ teaspoon black pepper
½ teaspoon ground cinnamon
½ teaspoon ground cumin
¼ teaspoon ground nutmeg
¼ teaspoon ground allspice
¼ teaspoon dried thyme leaves
3 cups water
3 ounces (about ⅓ cup) raisins
½ cup almond slivers, toasted (see Note)
3 cups hot cooked white rice

Place a 12-inch nonstick skillet over high heat for 1 minute. Add beef, brown, and, using a slotted spoon, transfer to paper towels to drain. Reduce heat to medium-high, add onion to skillet, and cook for 4 minutes or until onion is translucent. Add garlic, serrano, tomatoes, salt, bay leaf, black pepper, cinnamon, cumin, nutmeg, allspice, thyme, and water. Bring to a boil, reduce heat, and simmer, uncovered, for 15 minutes or until thickened slightly. Remove from heat and let stand, uncovered, for 10 minutes. Reheat over low heat before serving. At serving time, toss raisins and almonds with rice and spoon beef mixture over rice.

Makes about 4 cups

SUGGESTED GARNISH: Additional toasted slivered almonds

Cook's Note: Be sure to use almond slivers, not almond slices, for the best texture and flavor. To toast them, preheat broiler. Place the almond slivers in a broiler pan and broil no closer than 5 inches from the heat source for 30 seconds to 1 minute or until just beginning to brown. Be careful not to let them burn.

Hot and Hurried Pantry Beef Chili*

This low-fat chili is a very popular weeknight meal at our house. Served with tortilla chips, sour cream, and bottled salsa, it's a favorite of kids as well as grown-ups.

- 1 pound lean ground round
- 2 10-ounce cans diced tomatoes with green chiles, undrained
- 1 15-ounce can dark red kidney beans, rinsed and drained
- 2 tablespoons ketchup
- 1 tablespoon beef bouillon granules
- 2 teaspoons chili powder
- $\frac{1}{2}$ teaspoon ground cumin
- $1\frac{1}{2}$ cups water
- $1\frac{1}{2}$ teaspoons Worcestershire sauce

Place a dutch oven (preferably cast iron) over medium-high heat for 1 minute. Add beef, brown, and, using a slotted spoon, transfer to paper towels to drain. Return meat to pot and add remaining ingredients. Bring to a boil, reduce heat, and simmer, uncovered, for 25 minutes. Flavors improve if chili stands 30 minutes, uncovered. Reheat over low heat before serving.

Makes about 5 cups

SUGGESTED GARNISH: Baked low-fat tortilla chips, nonfat sour cream, and your favorite bottled salsa

Fajita Beef Chili with Monterey Wedges and Pico de Gallo

Marinated sirloin, peppers, and onions are quick-cooked and combined with seasoned black beans to create a savory smoked chili. This is served with baked tortilla wedges covered in melted Monterey Jack cheese.

PICO DE GALLO

- 2 fresh poblano chiles, stemmed, seeded, and chopped fine
- 3 fresh serrano chiles, stemmed, seeded, and chopped fine
- $\frac{1}{2}$ cup finely chopped red onion
- $1\frac{1}{2}$ cups finely chopped tomato
- $\frac{1}{2}$ cup peeled, seeded, and finely chopped cucumber
- $\frac{1}{4}$ cup finely chopped fresh cilantro or parsley leaves
- 2 tablespoons extra-virgin olive or vegetable oil

2 tablespoons red wine vinegar
1 tablespoon fresh lime juice
Salt and black pepper to taste

CHILI

¾ pound boneless top sirloin, cut into
 ½-inch pieces
2 cups slivered green bell pepper
2 cups slivered yellow onion
3 jalapeño chiles, seeded and chopped
⅓ cup reduced-sodium soy sauce
1 tablespoon A.1. steak sauce
2 garlic cloves, minced
½ teaspoon black pepper
1 15-ounce can black beans, rinsed and
 drained
4 plum tomatoes, chopped
1½ cups water
1½ teaspoons chili powder
2 tablespoons extra-virgin olive oil
4 6-inch corn or flour tortillas
1 cup (about ¼ pound) shredded Monterey
 Jack cheese with or without jalapeños

MAKE THE PICO DE GALLO

Mix together all ingredients and let stand at
room temperature for 1 hour.

MAKE THE CHILI

Preheat oven to 475°F. Combine beef, green
pepper, onion, chiles, soy sauce, steak sauce,
garlic, and black pepper in a bowl and toss to
blend thoroughly. Marinate at room temperature for 15 minutes, stirring occasionally.

While meat mixture is marinating, combine
beans, tomatoes, water, and chili powder in a
medium saucepan and stir gently but thoroughly. Bring to a boil over high heat, reduce
heat, and simmer for 5 minutes. Remove from
heat and set aside.

Place 1 tablespoon of the oil in a 10-inch skillet (preferably cast iron) and heat over high
heat for 2 minutes. Add half the meat mixture,
immediately reduce heat to medium-high, and
cook for 2–3 minutes or until liquid has evaporated and a glaze appears. Using a slotted
spoon, transfer to a bowl. Brown remaining
meat in remaining oil. Return first batch of
beef to skillet and add bean mixture. Stir and
cook for 1–2 minutes more to heat thoroughly.
Remove from heat.

Place tortillas on a baking sheet, top with
cheese, and bake for 3–4 minutes or until
cheese melts. Cut into wedges and serve immediately with chili, passing pico de gallo at the
table.

*Makes about 4 cups chili, about 2 cups pico de
gallo*

SUGGESTED GARNISH: Fresh lime wedges

Beef and Macaroni Chili*

This chili is a real child pleaser. Mild, sweetly spiced ground beef and beans are tossed with elbow macaroni noodles for a meal that's both easy to make and fun to eat.

1 pound lean ground round
2 cups chopped yellow onion
1 cup chopped green bell pepper
1 8-ounce can tomato sauce
2 tablespoons chili powder
1½ teaspoons ground cumin
¾ teaspoon ground cinnamon
¼ teaspoon ground allspice
⅛ teaspoon black pepper
¼ teaspoon salt or to taste
1½ teaspoons sugar
2 cups water
1 15-ounce can dark red kidney beans, rinsed and drained
¼ pound (about 1⅓ cups) dried elbow macaroni
1 teaspoon paprika

Coat a dutch oven (preferably cast iron) with low-calorie cooking spray and heat over high heat for 1 minute. Add beef, onion, and green pepper and cook until meat is no longer pink and liquid has evaporated. Add tomato sauce, chili powder, cumin, cinnamon, allspice, pepper, salt, sugar, and water. Bring to a boil, reduce heat, and simmer, uncovered, for 7 minutes. Add beans and simmer, covered, for 20 minutes.

While chili is cooking, cook noodles according to package directions, drain well, rinse quickly, and drain again. Toss with chili, cover, and let stand for 10 minutes. Reheat over low heat. Salt to taste, add paprika, and serve immediately.

Makes 6 cups

SUGGESTED GARNISH: Shredded sharp cheddar cheese (low-fat or nonfat if desired)

Cook's Note: This can be made ahead without the macaroni and simply reheated and tossed with freshly cooked pasta at serving time.

Red and Green Chili on Yellow Rice

A quick skillet dish with slow-simmered taste, this chili gets its rich flavor from fresh garlic, green chiles, tomatoes, and oregano leaves. It's served over Spanish rice tossed with olive oil.

1 pound ground chuck

4 garlic cloves, minced

2 4-ounce cans chopped green chiles, rinsed and drained

1 14½-ounce can diced tomatoes, undrained

2 14½-ounce cans beef broth (not condensed)

½ teaspoon dried oregano leaves

1¼ teaspoons sugar

1 5-ounce package Spanish-seasoned yellow rice

2 tablespoons extra-virgin olive oil

Heat a 12-inch nonstick skillet over medium-high heat for 1 minute. Add beef and garlic, brown, and, using a slotted spoon, transfer to paper towels to drain. Dry skillet with paper towels and return beef to skillet. Add green chiles, tomatoes and their juices, broth, oregano, and sugar. Bring to a boil, reduce heat to low, and simmer, uncovered, for 20 minutes.

While chili is simmering, cook rice according to package directions with 1 tablespoon of the oil. When chili is cooked, stir remaining oil into chili mixture and spoon over rice. Flavors will be at their peak when chili is served immediately after adding oil.

Makes 4 cups chili, about 2½ cups rice

SUGGESTED GARNISH: Shredded Monterey Jack and hot pepper cheeses

Lebanese Beef and Onion Chili with Toasted Pecans

Ground chuck and onions are flavored with cinnamon, chili powder, and cumin, served over steaming white rice, and topped with toasted pecans.

2 pounds ground chuck

6 cups chopped yellow onion

¼ cup chili powder

1 tablespoon plus 1 teaspoon ground
   cinnamon

2 teaspoons ground cumin

1 tablespoon sugar

2 teaspoons salt

½ teaspoon black pepper

2 teaspoons Worcestershire sauce

1 quart water

3–4 cups hot cooked white rice

¾ cup pecan pieces, toasted (see Note)

Heat a dutch oven (preferably cast iron) over medium-high heat for 1 minute. Add half the beef and half the onion, cook for 5–8 minutes or until onion is translucent, and, using a slotted spoon, transfer to paper towels to drain. Repeat with remaining beef and onion. Return beef and onion to dutch oven and add remaining ingredients except rice and pecans. Bring to a boil, reduce heat, and simmer, uncovered, for 30 minutes. Remove from heat and let stand, uncovered, for 10 minutes. Reheat over low heat before serving. At serving time, spoon over rice and top with pecans.

Makes about 6 cups

SUGGESTED GARNISH: Chopped scallions

Cook's Note: To toast the pecans, preheat broiler. Place the pecan pieces in a broiler pan and broil no closer than 5 inches from the heat source for 30 seconds to 1 minute or just until they begin to brown.

Thick Red and Black Bean Beef Chili

Here's a chili that requires almost no preparation time. Your favorite salsa combines with yellow corn, black and red beans, ground beef, and seasonings.

½ pound ground chuck

1 cup frozen corn kernels

1 15-ounce can black beans, rinsed and
   drained

1 15-ounce can red beans, rinsed and
   drained

1 cup extra-mild thick and chunky salsa

3 cups beef broth (not condensed)

1 tablespoon chili powder

2 teaspoons ground cumin

Heat a dutch oven (preferably cast iron) over medium-high heat for 1 minute. Add beef, brown, and, using a slotted spoon, transfer to paper towels to drain. Return beef to pot and add remaining ingredients except 1 teaspoon of the cumin. Bring to a boil, reduce heat to low, and simmer, uncovered, for 20 minutes.

Transfer 1 cup of the chili to a blender and blend until smooth. Return puree to dutch oven, add remaining teaspoon of cumin, stir to blend thoroughly, and let stand, uncovered, for 20 minutes to thicken slightly. Reheat over low heat and serve immediately.

Makes 5 cups

Suggested garnish: Additional chunky salsa

Beef and Two-Bean Chili with Soy*

A soup-style chili of fresh garlic, tomatoes, chiles, and garbanzo and dark red kidney beans, this dish gets its unique flavor from fresh parsley and soy sauce, added just prior to serving.

1/2 pound lean ground round
4 garlic cloves, minced
1/2 cup chopped yellow onion

1 10-ounce can diced tomatoes with green chiles, undrained
1 tablespoon beef bouillon granules
1 1/2 teaspoons ground cumin
1 teaspoon dried oregano leaves
1 cup canned garbanzo beans, rinsed and drained
1 cup canned dark red kidney beans, rinsed and drained
1/4 cup chopped fresh parsley
5 cups water
2 tablespoons reduced-sodium soy sauce
1/2 teaspoon sugar

Heat a dutch oven (preferably cast iron) over medium-high heat for 1 minute. Add beef and garlic, brown, and, using a slotted spoon, transfer to paper towels to drain. Reduce heat to medium, add onion to dutch oven, and sauté for 4 minutes or until translucent. Add tomatoes and chiles with their liquid, bouillon granules, cumin, oregano, garbanzo and kidney beans, 2 tablespoons of the parsley, and water. Bring to a boil, reduce heat, and simmer, uncovered, for 20 minutes. Remove from heat and stir in remaining 2 tablespoons parsley, soy sauce, and sugar. Stir and let stand, uncovered, for 10 minutes. Reheat over low heat.

Makes about 6 cups

Suggested garnish: Fresh parsley sprigs

Friday Night Taco-Stacked Chili

A delightfully fun and quick meal, this chili is surrounded by tortilla chips, topped with melted cheese, and stacked high with shredded lettuce, tomatoes, salsa, sour cream, onions, olives, and cilantro.

1 pound lean ground round
1 14½-ounce can beef broth (not condensed)
2 tablespoons tomato paste
2 tablespoons chili powder
1 tablespoon ground cumin
½ teaspoon sugar
¼ teaspoon cayenne pepper
⅛ teaspoon black pepper
1 15-ounce can dark red kidney beans, rinsed and drained
Tortilla chips
1 cup (about ¼ pound) grated sharp cheddar cheese
2 cups shredded lettuce
2 plum tomatoes, chopped
¼ cup finely chopped yellow onion
½ cup bottled salsa
½ cup sour cream
1 3.8-ounce can sliced black olives, drained
¼ cup chopped fresh cilantro leaves (optional)

Preheat oven to 350°F. Coat a 12-inch nonstick skillet with low-calorie cooking spray and heat over medium-high heat for 1 minute. Add beef and brown. While meat is browning, combine broth, tomato paste, chili powder, cumin, sugar, cayenne, and black pepper in a mixing bowl. Whisk until well blended and set aside. Using a slotted spoon, transfer meat to paper towels to drain. Pour off excess grease from skillet and return beef to pan along with broth mixture and beans. Bring to a boil, reduce heat, and simmer, uncovered, for 15 minutes.

Spoon chili into four individual ovenproof bowls or one 8″ × 12″ baking dish. Place chips around outer edges of bowls or baking dish, top chili mixture and edges of chips with cheese, and place in oven for 5 minutes or until cheese is melted. Remove from oven and top with lettuce, tomatoes, onion, salsa, sour cream, olives, and cilantro (if desired). Serve immediately.

Makes 4 cups

SUGGESTED GARNISH: Pickled jalapeño slices

Corn Bread-Crusted Mexican Chili Pizza

Teenagers—my own and their friends—are especially fond of this dish. Refrigerated corn bread dough is rolled out to form a bottom crust and topped with chili, Monterey Jack, chiles, olives, tomatoes, and cheddar cheese.

1 pound lean ground round

¼ cup chili powder

1½ tablespoons ground cumin

½ teaspoon salt

1 11.5-ounce package refrigerated corn bread twist dough

1½ cups (about 6 ounces) grated Monterey Jack cheese

1 4-ounce can green chiles, rinsed and drained

1 3.8-ounce can sliced black olives, drained

2 plum tomatoes, seeded and chopped

½ cup (about 2 ounces) grated sharp cheddar cheese

Preheat oven to 375°F. Heat a 10-inch skillet (preferably cast iron) over high heat for 1 minute. Add beef, chili powder, cumin, and salt and brown beef.

Coat a 9″ × 13″ baking dish with cooking spray. Carefully remove wrapping from dough and gently unroll onto lightly floured surface, trying not to split dough. Roll out to an 11″ × 15″ sheet and place in baking dish, lightly pressing dough into sides of pan.

Spoon beef mixture over crust and spread evenly. Sprinkle with Monterey Jack, then green chiles, black olives, and tomatoes. Place in oven and bake for 18 minutes. Remove, sprinkle with cheddar, and let stand, uncovered, for 5 minutes to let cheese melt slowly.

Makes 4–6 servings

SUGGESTED GARNISH: Sour cream and your favorite bottled salsa

Cook's Note: If dough splits, simply work with it in sections, fitting them snugly yet evenly into the baking dish.

Smoked Beef Chili with Red Beans

The concentrated flavor of sun-dried tomatoes combined with the smoky taste of steak sauce gives this dish its rich, satisfying appeal.

8 sun-dried tomatoes
2 cups boiling water
2 pounds ground chuck
2 cups chopped yellow onion
2 cups chopped green bell pepper
2 garlic cloves, minced
2 tablespoons chili powder
1 teaspoon ground cumin
1 teaspoon dried oregano leaves
½–¾ teaspoon cayenne pepper
½ teaspoon black pepper
2 14½-ounce cans beef broth (not
   condensed)
¼ cup A.1. steak sauce
1 15-ounce can light red kidney beans,
   rinsed and drained

Place tomatoes in a bowl, cover with boiling water, and let stand for 5 minutes. Remove (reserve tomato water), chop, and set aside.

Place beef in a dutch oven (preferably cast iron) and brown over medium-high heat. Using a slotted spoon, transfer to paper towels to drain. Add onion, green pepper, and garlic to any pan drippings in dutch oven and cook for 4 minutes or until onion is translucent. Return beef to dutch oven and add chili powder, cumin, oregano, cayenne, and black pepper. Cook for 2 minutes. Add broth, tomatoes and tomato water, and steak sauce and bring to a boil. Reduce heat to low and simmer, uncovered, for 20 minutes. Add beans and simmer for 10 minutes more. Remove from heat and let stand, uncovered, for at least 20 minutes. Reheat before serving, adding a little water to thin the chili if desired.

Makes about 8 cups

SUGGESTED GARNISH:
Sour cream topped
with chopped
tomatoes

Enchilada Beef Chili with Cheese

Beef is simmered in a red chile sauce, combined with corn tortilla strips, and topped with two cheeses for a quick, hearty meal.

1 pound ground chuck

1 cup chopped yellow onion

2 garlic cloves, minced

⅓ cup chili powder

1 tablespoon ground cumin

3 cups canned beef broth (not condensed)

1 6-ounce can tomato paste

1 teaspoon sugar

1 cup water

4 6-inch corn tortillas, cut into ½″ × 1″ pieces

½ cup (about 2 ounces) grated sharp cheddar cheese

½ cup (about 2 ounces) grated Monterey Jack cheese

Place beef, onion, and garlic in a dutch oven (preferably cast iron) over medium-high heat and brown. Add chili powder and cumin. Cook for 2 minutes. Add broth, tomato paste, sugar, and water and stir until well blended. Bring to a boil, reduce heat to low, cover tightly, and cook for 45 minutes. Add tortilla strips and cook, uncovered, for 5 minutes. Remove from heat, top with both cheeses, and let stand, uncovered, for 10 minutes to melt cheese. Reheat over low heat.

Makes 6–7 cups

SUGGESTED GARNISH: Sour cream and finely chopped red onion

Cook's Note: Adding sugar to the chili takes the sharpness out of the dish, making it more mellow.

Pork Chilies

▼▼▼

Sausage, White Bean, and Pasta Chili

This is a nourishing, stick-to-the-ribs chili of mild Italian sausage, tomatoes, chiles, white beans, and pasta shells.

- 1 pound mild Italian sausage, casings removed
- 2 14½-ounce cans diced tomatoes, undrained
- 2 14½-ounce cans chicken broth (not condensed)
- 2 4-ounce cans chopped green chiles, rinsed and drained
- 2 teaspoons paprika
- ¼ teaspoon cayenne pepper
- 2 tablespoons ground cumin
- 1 15-ounce can navy beans, rinsed and drained
- ½ cup small pasta shells, cooked (makes about 1 cup)
- 2 tablespoons extra-virgin olive oil

Place a dutch oven (preferably cast iron) over high heat for 1 minute. Add sausage, brown, and, using a slotted spoon, transfer to paper towels to drain. Pour off excess grease from dutch oven. Return sausage to pot and add tomatoes and their liquid, broth, green chiles, paprika, cayenne, and cumin. Bring to a boil, reduce heat, and simmer, uncovered, for 25 minutes. Remove from heat, stir in beans and pasta, and mix gently but thoroughly. Gently stir in oil and let stand, uncovered, for 10 minutes before serving. Reheat over low heat.

Makes about 8 cups

SUGGESTED GARNISH: Crumbled feta cheese and chopped fresh parsley

Italian Black Sausage Chili with Sour Cream and Peperoncini

Old World, slow-cooked flavors are infused in this black bean chili. It features a mellow, mouth-watering combination of mild Italian sausage, onions, peppers, garlic, tomatoes, and fennel.

- 1 tablespoon extra-virgin olive oil
- 1 pound mild Italian sausage, casings removed
- 1 cup chopped yellow onion
- ½ cup chopped green bell pepper

4 garlic cloves, minced
2 15-ounce cans black beans, rinsed and
  drained
1 quart water
1 10-ounce can condensed beef broth
1 14½-ounce can diced tomatoes,
  undrained
½ teaspoon dried oregano leaves
¼ teaspoon hot red pepper flakes
¼ teaspoon fennel seeds
Sour cream
Peperoncini, chopped

Place oil in a dutch oven (preferably cast iron) and heat over medium-high heat for 1 minute. Add sausage, brown, and, using a slotted spoon, drain on paper towels. Pour off excess grease from dutch oven, reduce heat to medium, and add onion, bell pepper, and garlic. Cook for 4 minutes or until onion is translucent. Add beans and cook for 2 minutes. Add water, broth, tomatoes and their liquid, oregano, red pepper flakes, fennel, and sausage. Bring to a boil, reduce heat, and simmer, uncovered, for 20 minutes. Remove from heat and let stand, uncovered, for 15 minutes before serving. Flavors improve if chili is refrigerated overnight or for at least 4 hours. Reheat over low heat. Garnish with sour cream and peperoncini.

Makes 8 cups

Mild Garbanzo-Bacon Chili

This is a mellow, smoky-flavored chili.

8 slices bacon
3 cups chopped yellow onion
4 garlic cloves, minced
2 jalapeño chiles, seeded and minced
2 14½-ounce cans chicken broth (not
  condensed)
2 15-ounce cans garbanzo beans, rinsed
  and drained
1 tablespoon ground cumin
½ cup finely chopped green bell pepper

Place a dutch oven (preferably cast iron) over medium-high heat, add bacon, and cook until crisp. Transfer bacon to paper towels to drain, then crumble and set aside. Discard all but 1 tablespoon of the bacon drippings from dutch oven and add onion, garlic, and jalapeños. Cook for 4 minutes or until onion is translucent. Add broth and bring to a boil. Add beans, cumin, and bacon and return to a boil. Reduce heat and simmer, uncovered, for 25 minutes. Add green pepper and simmer for 5 minutes more. Remove from heat and let stand, uncovered, for 5 minutes to absorb flavors.

Makes about 4 cups

SUGGESTED GARNISH: Additional minced jalapeño and finely chopped bell pepper

Yellow Corn Chili with Bacon*

A wholesome, great-tasting chili, this combines sweet yellow corn, dark red kidney beans, a touch of bacon, and chili seasonings.

 2 slices bacon
 ½ cup chopped yellow onion
 3 cups fresh or frozen yellow corn kernels
 2 garlic cloves, minced
 1 tablespoon chili powder
 ½ teaspoon dried oregano leaves
 1 15-ounce can dark red kidney beans, rinsed and drained
 3 cups water
 1 teaspoon salt
 ⅛ teaspoon black pepper
 ½ teaspoon ground cumin

Heat a dutch oven (preferably cast iron) over medium-high heat for 1 minute. Add bacon, cook until crisp, and transfer to paper towels to drain. Crumble and set aside. Discard all but 1 tablespoon of the bacon drippings from dutch oven, add onion, and cook, stirring, for 3 minutes or until edges begin to brown. Add corn, garlic, chili powder, and oregano. Cook for 4 minutes or until all the liquid is absorbed. Add beans, water, ½ teaspoon of the salt, pepper, and crumbled bacon. Bring to a boil, reduce heat, and simmer 15 minutes, uncovered. Stir in cumin and remaining ½ teaspoon

salt and let stand, uncovered, for 10 minutes. Reheat over low heat before serving.

Makes about 5 cups

Suggested garnish: Cilantro leaves

Bacon, Snapper, and Tomato Chili*

This distinctive chili combines red snapper, bacon, whole jalapeños, and chili seasonings for a great spring or summer meal.

 2 slices bacon
 1 cup chopped yellow onion
 2 garlic cloves, minced
 1 teaspoon dried oregano leaves
 1½ teaspoons chili powder
 1 14½-ounce can diced tomatoes, undrained
 1½ cups water
 2 whole fresh jalapeño chiles
 1 pound red snapper fillets, cut into 1-inch pieces
 ½ teaspoon ground cumin
 Salt to taste
 2 tablespoons chopped fresh cilantro leaves

Place bacon in a dutch oven (preferably cast iron) and cook over medium-high heat until crisp. Transfer to paper towels to drain, then crumble and set aside. Discard all but 1 tablespoon of the bacon drippings from dutch oven and add onion and garlic. Cook for 4 minutes or until onion is translucent. Add oregano and chili powder and cook for 1 minute more. Add tomatoes and their liquid, water, and jalapeños and bring to a boil. Add snapper, bacon, and cumin. Bring just to a boil, reduce heat, and simmer for 5 minutes. Stir in salt, to taste, and cilantro and serve immediately.

Makes 5–6 cups

Suggested garnish: Diagonally sliced scallions

Hot Black Bean and Corn Chili

A colorful chili with hot and spicy sausage, this dish also offers up sweet yellow corn, black beans, tomatoes, and cilantro, smothered with melted cheddar cheese.

- ¾ pound hot Italian sausage, casings removed
- 1 cup fresh or frozen corn kernels
- 1 15-ounce can black beans, rinsed and drained
- 1 14½-ounce can beef broth (not condensed)
- 1 14½-ounce can diced tomatoes, undrained
- 1 tablespoon chili powder
- 1 teaspoon ground cumin
- 2 tablespoons chopped fresh cilantro leaves
- 1 cup (about ¼ pound) grated sharp cheddar cheese

Preheat broiler. Coat a dutch oven (preferably cast iron) with low-calorie cooking spray and heat over medium-high heat for 1 minute. Add sausage, brown, and, using a slotted spoon, transfer to paper towels to drain. Dry dutch oven with a paper towel and return sausage to dutch oven along with corn, beans, broth, tomatoes and their liquid, chili powder, and cumin. Bring to a boil, reduce heat, and simmer, uncovered, for 25 minutes. Remove from heat, stir in cilantro, sprinkle cheese over top, and place under broiler until cheese has melted and begun to brown slightly. Flavors will be at their peak if chili is served immediately.

Makes 5–6 cups

Suggested garnish: Additional corn kernels, tossed with finely chopped cilantro leaves

Louisiana Bayou Chili with Hot Pepper Sauce

A touch of bacon adds rich flavor to this chili of onions, peppers, corn, tomatoes, okra, and black-eyed peas.

4 slices bacon
1 cup chopped yellow onion
1 cup green bell pepper
2 garlic cloves, minced
3 cups water
1 tablespoon beef or chicken bouillon
   granules
1 cup fresh or frozen corn kernels
4 plum tomatoes, seeded and chopped
8 fresh okra pods, cut into ½-inch pieces
1 tablespoon chili powder
1½ teaspoons ground cumin
¼ teaspoon cayenne pepper
¼ teaspoon dried
   thyme leaves
1 bay leaf
1 15-ounce can black-eyed peas, rinsed and
   drained
Louisiana hot pepper sauce

Heat a dutch oven (preferably cast iron) over medium-high heat for 1 minute. Add bacon and cook until crisp. Transfer to paper towels to drain, then crumble and set aside. Discard all but 2 tablespoons of the drippings from dutch oven and add onion, green pepper, and garlic. Cook for 4 minutes or until onion is translucent. Add water and bouillon granules, bring to a boil, and add corn, tomatoes, okra, chili powder, cumin, cayenne, thyme, and bay leaf. Return to a boil, reduce heat, and simmer, covered, for 10–12 minutes. Add peas, bacon, and hot pepper sauce and simmer, uncovered, for 5 minutes more. Remove from heat and let stand, uncovered, for 30 minutes. Reheat over low heat before serving.

Makes 4 cups

Suggested garnish: Chopped pimiento

Poultry Chilies

▼▼▼

Cajun Chicken, Sausage, and Bean Chili

A great cold-weather chili, this requires almost no effort to prepare. Sausage, chicken, onions, beans, and seasonings are cooked with a mix of Cajun-flavored red and white beans and rice.

½ pound mild Italian sausage, casings removed

¾ pound skinless, boneless chicken breasts, cut into ½-inch pieces

1 cup chopped yellow onion

2 quarts water

1 15-ounce can white beans, rinsed and drained

1 7.4-ounce box Uncle Ben's Red Beans and Rice mix

½ teaspoon dried thyme leaves

1 tablespoon chili powder

1 teaspoon ground cumin

½ teaspoon salt or to taste

Place a dutch oven (preferably cast iron) over medium-high heat, add sausage, and brown. Using a slotted spoon, transfer meat to paper towels to drain. Pour off excess grease from dutch oven and add chicken. Cook for 4 minutes or until just beginning to brown, and, using a slotted spoon, transfer to a bowl. Add onion to dutch oven and cook for 4 minutes or until translucent. Add water and bring to a boil. Add white beans, rice mix, thyme, sausage, and chicken and return to a boil. Reduce heat and simmer, covered, for 25 minutes. Remove from heat, add chili powder, cumin, and salt, and let stand, uncovered, for 20 minutes. Reheat over low heat and serve.

Makes 8–10 cups

SUGGESTED GARNISH:
Chopped pimiento or pimiento strips

Great Northern White Bean and Chicken Chili*

1 tablespoon extra-virgin olive oil
1 pound skinless, boneless chicken breasts, cut into ½-inch pieces
2 cups chopped yellow onion
1 cup chopped green bell pepper
2 garlic cloves, minced
4 14½-ounce cans chicken broth (not condensed)
2 15-ounce cans Great Northern beans, rinsed and drained
1 tablespoon ground cumin
Black pepper to taste

Place oil in a dutch oven (preferably cast iron) and heat over medium-high heat for 1 minute. Add chicken, cook until no longer pink (3–4 minutes), and, using a slotted spoon, transfer to a bowl. To any pan drippings in dutch oven, add onion, green pepper, and garlic. Cook for 5 minutes or until onion is translucent and beginning to turn golden. Add broth, beans, 2 teaspoons of the cumin, and chicken and any accumulated juices. Bring to a boil, reduce heat, and simmer, uncovered, for 20 minutes. Remove from heat, stir in remaining teaspoon of cumin and the black pepper, and let stand, uncovered, for 30 minutes to thicken slightly. Reheat over low heat before serving.

Makes about 7 cups

SUGGESTED GARNISH: Thinly sliced roasted red bell pepper

Skillet Chicken, Rice, and Red Bean Cumin Chili*

This is a hearty, healthy dish of tomato- and chile-seasoned chicken and vegetables cooked with rice and beans.

1 cup cooked diced chicken
¾ cup chopped yellow onion
¾ cup chopped green bell pepper
½ cup tomato sauce
2 garlic cloves, minced
¼ teaspoon hot red pepper flakes
3 14½-ounce cans chicken broth (not condensed)
1 cup rinsed and drained canned red beans
2 teaspoons chili powder
1 teaspoon paprika
½ cup converted rice
½ teaspoon ground cumin
¼ cup chopped fresh cilantro leaves

In a dutch oven (preferably cast iron), combine all ingredients except rice, cumin, and cilantro.

Bring to a boil, stir in rice, and return to a boil. Reduce heat, cover tightly, and simmer for 20 minutes. Remove from heat, stir in cumin and cilantro, cover, and let stand for 5 minutes before serving.

Makes 5–6 cups

SUGGESTED GARNISH: Your favorite bottled hot pepper sauce

Italian Turkey and Bean Chili*

This savory chili is a delicious blend of sausage, onions, green peppers, zucchini, tomatoes, dark red kidney beans, and parsley.

6 ounces turkey bulk sausage
½ cup finely chopped yellow onion
½ cup finely chopped green bell pepper
2 cups thinly sliced zucchini
1 14½-ounce can diced tomatoes, undrained
1 15-ounce can dark red kidney beans, rinsed and drained
1 tablespoon beef bouillon granules
1–2 tablespoons chili powder, to taste
½ teaspoon sugar
3 cups water
¼ cup chopped fresh parsley
1 tablespoon extra-virgin olive oil
½ cup (about 2 ounces) grated mozzarella cheese

Coat a dutch oven (preferably cast iron) with low-calorie cooking spray and heat over medium-high heat for 1 minute. Add sausage and brown, crumbling with a fork. Using a slotted spoon, transfer to paper towels to drain. Add onion and green pepper to pan drippings and cook for 4 minutes or until onion is translucent. Add zucchini, tomatoes and their liquid, beans, bouillon granules, chili powder, sugar, and water. Bring to a boil, add sausage, and return to a boil. Reduce heat and simmer, uncovered, for 25 minutes. Remove from heat, add parsley and olive oil, and stir gently. Let stand, uncovered, for 30 minutes. Reheat over low heat before serving. Top each serving with grated mozzarella.

Makes about 4 cups

SUGGESTED GARNISH: Chopped Kalamata olives and parsley sprigs

Healthy Home-Style Turkey Chili with Beans*

This chili is packed with nutrition and fiber. The addition of extra cumin just before serving gives it a more pronounced flavor.

- 1 12-ounce package turkey bulk sausage
- 2 15-ounce cans dark red kidney beans, rinsed and drained
- 1 16-ounce can tomato sauce
- 2 cups hot tap water
- 1 1.2-ounce package chili seasoning
- 1½ teaspoons ground cumin

Coat a 12-inch nonstick skillet with low-calorie cooking spray and heat over medium-high heat for 1 minute. Add sausage and brown, crumbling with a fork. Using a slotted spoon, transfer to paper towels to drain. Dry skillet with a paper towel and return sausage to pan. Add remaining ingredients except cumin and stir to blend thoroughly. Bring to a boil, reduce heat to low, and simmer, uncovered, for 20 minutes. Remove from heat, add cumin, and let stand, uncovered, for 30 minutes before serving. Reheat over low heat.

Makes about 6 cups

SUGGESTED GARNISH: Thinly sliced avocado and lime wedges

Turkey Chili on Bow Tie Pasta*

Served over pasta, this chili has an appetizing Mexican "cacciatore" flavor.

- 1 tablespoon extra-virgin olive oil
- 2 cups chopped yellow onion
- 1 cup chopped green bell pepper
- ½ pound skinless, boneless turkey or chicken breasts, cut into ½-inch pieces
- 1 14½-ounce can diced tomatoes
- 1 cup bottled mild salsa
- 1 cup water
- 1½ tablespoons chili powder
- 1½ teaspoons ground cumin
- 4 cups cooked bow tie pasta

Place oil in a 12-inch nonstick skillet and heat over medium-high heat for 1 minute. Add onion and green pepper and cook for 4 minutes or until onion is translucent. Add turkey and brown. Add tomatoes and their liquid, salsa, water, 1 tablespoon of the chili powder, and ½ teaspoon of the cumin. Bring to a boil, reduce heat, cover tightly, and simmer for 20 minutes. Stir in remaining 1½ teaspoons chili powder and remaining teaspoon of cumin. Let stand, covered, for 20 minutes. Reheat over low heat. Serve over hot pasta.

Makes about 4 cups

SUGGESTED GARNISH: Shredded Monterey Jack with hot pepper cheese

Vegetable Chilies

▼▼▼

Southwestern Vegetarian Chili*

This dish is not for the faint of appetite! It features a hearty, satisfying blend of dark red and black beans, golden onions, peppers, fresh garlic, and tomatoes. Seasoned with smoky steak sauce and flavorful spices, it's topped with cilantro, sour cream, and chopped red onion.

2 tablespoons extra-virgin olive oil
½ cup chopped green bell pepper
½ cup chopped yellow onion
2 garlic cloves, minced
1 tablespoon chili powder
1 tablespoon ground cumin
1 14½-ounce can diced tomatoes, undrained
1 15-ounce can dark red kidney beans, rinsed and drained
1 15-ounce can black beans, rinsed and drained
2 tablespoons A.1. steak sauce
2 cups water
¼ teaspoon salt or to taste

¼ cup chopped fresh cilantro leaves
Nonfat sour cream
Finely chopped red onion

Place 1 tablespoon of the oil in a dutch oven (preferably cast iron) and heat over medium-high heat for 1 minute. Add green pepper, onion, and garlic and cook for 6 minutes or until onion begins to turn golden. Add chili powder and cumin and cook for 1 minute more. Add tomatoes and their liquid, kidney and black beans, steak sauce, water, and salt. Bring to a boil, reduce heat, and simmer, uncovered, for 20 minutes. Remove from heat, gently stir in remaining oil, and let stand, uncovered, for 10 minutes. Reheat over low heat. Top with cilantro leaves, sour cream, and red onion.

Makes about 5 cups

Cook's Note: If a thicker chili is desired, place 1 cup of the chili mixture in a blender and blend until smooth. Add to pot, stir into chili, and heat thoroughly before topping with cilantro, sour cream, and onion.

New Mexican Jalapeño Cheese Chili with Spinach

A Mexican chili based on cheddar cheese and green chiles, this dish features tomatoes, onions, peppers, leaf spinach, and rice.

- 1½ teaspoons extra-virgin olive oil
- 1 cup chopped yellow onion
- ½ cup chopped green bell pepper
- 2 garlic cloves, minced
- 1 tablespoon chili powder
- 1½ teaspoons ground cumin
- ½ teaspoon dried oregano leaves
- 5 cups regular canned chicken broth (not condensed)
- 1 cup canned diced tomatoes, undrained
- ½ cup converted rice
- 4 ounces Velveeta Mild Mexican Cheese
- 1 10-ounce package frozen leaf spinach, thawed and squeezed dry

Place oil in a dutch oven (preferably cast iron) and heat over medium-high heat for 1 minute. Add onion, green pepper, and garlic and cook for 4 minutes or until onion is translucent. Add chili powder, cumin, and oregano and cook for 1 minute more. Add broth and tomatoes with their liquid. Bring to a boil, add rice, and return to a boil. Reduce heat, cover tightly, and simmer for 25 minutes. Remove from heat, stir in cheese and spinach, cover, and let stand for 5 minutes to melt cheese. Stir, cover, and let stand for 5 minutes more to absorb flavors. If a thicker chili is desired, mix 2 tablespoons water with 2 teaspoons cornstarch until smooth. Add to the chili and cook for 2–3 minutes over medium heat or until slightly thickened.

Makes about 5–6 cups

SUGGESTED GARNISH: Chopped scallions

Black Bean Cumin Chili*

Deliciously simple, this classic chili features cumin-scented black beans, onions, and fresh garlic. It may be thickened by processing a portion of the mixture in a blender and adding it to the remaining chili while cooking.

- 1½ teaspoons extra-virgin olive oil
- 1 cup chopped yellow onion
- 2 garlic cloves, minced
- 2 15-ounce cans black beans, rinsed and drained
- 3 cups canned chicken broth (not condensed)

¼ teaspoon black pepper
1 tablespoon ground cumin
2 cups hot cooked rice

Place oil in a dutch oven (preferably cast iron) and heat over medium-high heat for 1 minute. Add onion and garlic and cook for 5–6 minutes or until edges begin to brown. Add beans, broth, and black pepper. Bring to a boil, reduce heat, cover tightly, and simmer for 25 minutes. Uncover, add cumin, and cook for 5 minutes longer. Flavors will be at their peak if chili is served immediately. Serve over rice.

Makes about 4 cups

SUGGESTED GARNISH: Lime wedges and finely chopped fresh Anaheim or New Mexican green chiles

Hearty Bean and Onion Chili*

Tender, golden onions and mild garbanzo beans complement dark red kidney beans and a variety of seasonings in this chili.

3 tablespoons extra-virgin olive oil
4 cups chopped yellow onion
4 garlic cloves, minced
1 15-ounce can garbanzo beans, rinsed and drained
1 15-ounce can dark red kidney beans, rinsed and drained
2 tablespoons chili powder
1½ teaspoons ground cumin
1 teaspoon paprika
¼ teaspoon cayenne
¼ teaspoon black pepper
2 14½-ounce cans beef broth (not condensed)
1½ cups water

Place 1½ tablespoons of the oil in a heavy 10-inch skillet (preferably cast iron) and heat over medium-high heat for 1 minute. Add half of the onion and garlic and cook for 12–14 minutes or until richly browned and caramelized. Transfer onion and garlic to a dutch oven and set aside. Repeat with remaining oil, onion, and garlic. Add garbanzo and kidney beans, chili powder, cumin, paprika, cayenne, and black pepper to dutch oven and cook for 1 minute. Add broth and water, bring to a boil, reduce heat, and simmer, uncovered, for 20 minutes. Remove from heat and let stand for 10–15 minutes to thicken slightly. Reheat over low heat if necessary.

Makes about 7 cups

SUGGESTED GARNISH: Thin strips of roasted red bell pepper

Cayenne Bean Chili

This thick, hearty kidney bean chili has a beef broth base. It's highly spiced with cayenne pepper and may be topped with smoked Gouda cheese and finely chopped red onion or simply served with oyster crackers.

2 tablespoons extra-virgin olive oil
2 garlic cloves, minced
1/2 cup chopped yellow onion
1/2 cup chopped scallion
1/4 cup chopped green bell pepper
1 1/2 tablespoons chili powder
1 teaspoon ground cumin
1/4 teaspoon dried oregano leaves
1 15-ounce can dark red kidney beans, rinsed and drained
3 cups canned beef broth (not condensed)
1/2 cup water
1/4–1/2 teaspoon cayenne pepper

Place 1 tablespoon of the oil in a dutch oven (preferably cast iron) and heat over medium-high heat for 1 minute. Add garlic and onion and cook for 4 minutes or until onion is translucent. Add remaining ingredients (except remaining tablespoon of oil) and bring to a boil. Reduce heat, cover tightly, and simmer for 25 minutes. Place 1/2 cup of the bean mixture in a blender and blend until smooth. Return puree to dutch oven and cook, uncovered, for 5 minutes longer. Remove from heat, stir in remaining oil, and let stand, uncovered, for 30 minutes to thicken slightly. Reheat over low heat.

Makes about 4 cups

SUGGESTED GARNISH: Shredded smoked Gouda and finely chopped red onion or oyster crackers

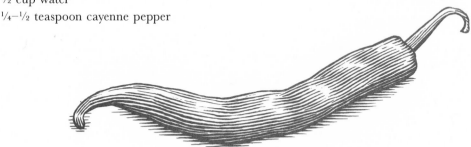

7
Chile Soups

Jalapeño Cheddar Soup with Bacon

This rich, thick, and very creamy chile cheese soup is seasoned with tender-cooked jalapeños, onion, green pepper, celery, garlic, cilantro, and bacon.

4 slices bacon

8 fresh jalapeño chiles, stemmed, seeded, and minced

1 cup chopped yellow onion

1 cup chopped green bell pepper

½ cup chopped celery

2 garlic cloves, minced

3 cups canned chicken broth (not condensed)

¼ cup flour

1 teaspoon paprika

2 cups (about ½ pound) shredded sharp cheddar cheese

2 cups half-and-half

¼ cup chopped fresh cilantro leaves or parsley (optional)

4 plum tomatoes, seeded and chopped

Place bacon in a dutch oven (preferably cast iron) over medium-high heat and cook until crisp. Transfer to paper towels to drain, then crumble and set aside. Discard all but 1 tablespoon of the bacon drippings from dutch oven and add jalapeños, onion, green pepper, celery, and garlic. Cook for 8 minutes or until onion is soft.

In a small mixing bowl, combine 1 cup of the broth and flour and whisk until smooth. Add flour mixture to dutch oven along with the remaining broth and paprika. Stir to blend thoroughly. Bring to a boil, reduce heat, and simmer, uncovered, for 15 minutes.

Remove from heat and slowly whisk in cheese, stirring until melted. Stir in half-and-half until well blended. Add cilantro, tomatoes, and bacon and stir to blend. Flavors will be at their peak if chile soup is served immediately.

Makes about 7 cups

SUGGESTED GARNISH: Small whole jalapeño chiles

Mediterranean Pepper Soup with Capers*

Chicken, mushrooms, onions, sweet red peppers, and zucchini are lightly browned and simmered in a chicken-based stock with small white beans, herbs, and chili seasonings. Fresh tomatoes, parsley, capers, and olive oil are added to give this chile soup its fresh, distinctive flavor.

2 tablespoons extra-virgin olive oil
¾ pound skinless, boneless chicken breasts
6 ounces (2 cups) fresh mushrooms, quartered
1 cup finely chopped yellow onion
1 cup finely chopped red bell pepper
8 garlic cloves, minced
3 14½-ounce cans reduced-sodium chicken broth (not condensed)
1 medium zucchini, diced (about 2 cups)
½ teaspoon dried oregano leaves
½ teaspoon hot red pepper flakes
1½ teaspoons chili powder
4 plum tomatoes, seeded and chopped
¾ cup chopped fresh parsley or cilantro
2 tablespoons tomato paste
1 cup rinsed and drained canned navy beans
1 tablespoon drained capers

Place 1 tablespoon of the oil in a dutch oven (preferably cast iron) and heat over medium-high heat for 1 minute. Add chicken and cook for 4 minutes. Turn and cook for 4 minutes more. Transfer to a plate. Add mushrooms to pan drippings in dutch oven and cook for 3 minutes. Add onion, red pepper, and garlic and cook for 4 minutes or until onion is translucent. Add broth, zucchini, oregano, red pepper flakes, and chili powder. Bring to a boil, reduce heat, and simmer, uncovered, for 15 minutes. Reheat over low heat.

While soup is simmering, cut chicken into ½-inch pieces and set aside. Add chicken, tomatoes, ½ cup of the parsley, tomato paste, and beans, stirring gently but thoroughly to blend. Bring to a boil, reduce heat, and simmer, uncovered, for 5 minutes.

Remove from heat, add remaining tablespoon of olive oil and capers and remaining ¼ cup parsley. Let stand, uncovered, for 10 minutes before serving. Reheat over low heat.

Makes 7–8 cups

SUGGESTED GARNISH: Thinly sliced provolone cheese

Cilantro Chicken and Rice Pepper Soup*

A fresh, light soup of chicken, salsa, and chili seasonings, with Spanish rice, cilantro, and olive oil added to heighten the flavors of the dish.

2 tablespoons extra-virgin olive oil
1 cup chopped yellow onion
½ cup chopped green bell pepper
2 garlic cloves, minced
1½ pounds skinless, boneless chicken
    breasts, cut into ½-inch pieces
2 14½-ounce cans reduced-sodium chicken
    broth (not condensed)
1 14½-ounce can beef broth (not
    condensed)
1 cup extra-mild thick and chunky bottled
    salsa
1 cup water
1 tablespoon chili powder
1 teaspoon ground cumin
4 cups cooked Spanish-seasoned yellow
    rice, no salt or oil added during
    cooking
Chopped fresh cilantro leaves

Place 1 tablespoon of the oil in a dutch oven (preferably cast iron) and heat over medium-high heat for 1 minute. Add onion, green pepper, and garlic and cook for 8 minutes or until onion is just beginning to brown. Add chicken and cook for 5–6 minutes or until no longer pink. Add chicken broth, beef broth, salsa, water, chili powder, and ½ teaspoon of the cumin. Bring to a boil, reduce heat, and simmer, uncovered, for 20 minutes.

Remove from heat, stir in remaining ½ teaspoon cumin and remaining tablespoon of olive oil, and let stand, uncovered, for 20 minutes before serving. Reheat over low heat. Stir in rice and top with chopped cilantro.

Makes 7–8 cups

SUGGESTED GARNISH: Shredded Monterey Jack with hot pepper cheese

Chile Rellenos Soup with Fresh Lime

Roasted poblanos stuffed with Monterey Jack cheese are baked quickly and served in a simple lima sopa, *a delightful chicken broth seasoned with fresh lime juice, olive oil, and cilantro.*

4 fresh poblano chiles
¼ pound Monterey Jack cheese, cut into
    4 long strips (½″ × 1″ × 2½″)
½ cup (about 2 ounces) grated Monterey
    Jack cheese
3 14½-ounce cans chicken broth (not
    condensed)
¼ cup fresh lime juice
1 tablespoon extra-virgin olive oil
¼ teaspoon chili powder
2 tablespoons chopped cilantro leaves
Lime wedges

Preheat broiler. Place poblano chiles on a foil-lined oven rack and broil 2–3 inches from heat source for 10–12 minutes or until completely blistered, turning occasionally. Transfer to a bowl of ice water and let stand for 5 minutes.

Reset oven to 400°F. When chiles have cooled, peel carefully, leaving them whole. Carefully cut off stems and remove seeds. Coat a non-stick baking sheet with cooking spray and place chiles on sheet. Fill each chile with a strip of cheese. Sprinkle grated cheese evenly over each chile, place in oven, and bake for 10 minutes or until cheese has melted inside.

While chiles are baking, place broth in a 2-quart saucepan and bring to a boil over high heat. Remove from heat, stir in lime juice and oil, and let stand for 2–3 minutes.

Remove chiles from oven, sprinkle with chili powder, and let stand for 5 minutes to allow cheese to set. Pour broth mixture into individual wide, shallow bowls. Using a flat spatula, carefully transfer cheese-stuffed chile to the center of each bowl. Sprinkle with cilantro and serve immediately with lime wedges.

Makes 4 servings

Suggested garnish: Chili powder

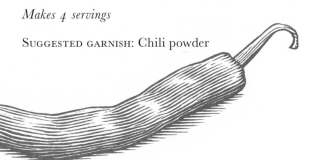

Hot Creamy Potato and Anaheim Chile Soup

Roasted Anaheim and poblano chiles add a mellow heat to this rich, satisfying soup.

6 fresh Anaheim or New Mexican green
    chiles
2 fresh poblano chiles
¼ cup butter
2 cups chopped yellow onion
3 garlic cloves, minced
2 14½-ounce cans chicken broth (not
    condensed)
¾ pound (about 2 medium) white
    potatoes, peeled and cubed
1 teaspoon dried oregano leaves
2 cups half-and-half
4 plum tomatoes, seeded and chopped
½ teaspoon ground cumin
¼ teaspoon salt or to taste

Preheat broiler. Place Anaheim and poblano chiles on a foil-lined oven rack and broil 2–3 inches from heat source for 10–12 minutes or until completely blistered, turning occasionally. Transfer to a bowl of ice water and let stand for 5 minutes. Peel chiles, remove stems, seeds, and membranes, and set aside.

Place butter in a dutch oven (preferably cast iron) and heat over medium heat until melted and beginning to bubble. Add onion and garlic and cook for 6–7 minutes or until onion is soft. Add broth and bring to a boil. Add potatoes, oregano, and roasted chiles. Return to a boil, reduce heat, and simmer, uncovered, for 20 minutes. Remove from heat.

One cup at a time, transfer soup to a blender and blend until smooth. Return puree to dutch oven and add half-and-half, tomatoes, cumin, and salt. Bring to a simmer over medium heat and cook, uncovered, for 8 minutes. Flavors will be at their peak if soup is served immediately.

Makes about 7 cups

SUGGESTED GARNISH: Additional roasted green chile strips or finely chopped fresh green chiles

Cook's Note: The soup can be made up to 8 hours in advance, and refrigerated, without the half-and-half, tomatoes, and cumin. At serving time, reheat over medium heat, slowly whisk in the half-and-half and cumin, gently stir in the tomatoes, and cook for 8 minutes.

Spicy Bean Soup

This soup offers a deliciously seasoned combination of dark red kidney beans simmered in beef broth, onions, and scallions.

2 tablespoons extra-virgin olive oil

4 garlic cloves, minced

1 cup chopped yellow onion

½ cup chopped green bell pepper

1 cup chopped scallion

3 tablespoons chili powder

2 teaspoons ground cumin

½ teaspoon dried oregano leaves

½ teaspoon hot red pepper flakes or to taste

2 15-ounce cans dark red kidney beans, rinsed and drained

3 14½-ounce cans beef broth (not condensed)

1 cup water

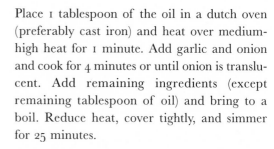

Place 1 tablespoon of the oil in a dutch oven (preferably cast iron) and heat over medium-high heat for 1 minute. Add garlic and onion and cook for 4 minutes or until onion is translucent. Add remaining ingredients (except remaining tablespoon of oil) and bring to a boil. Reduce heat, cover tightly, and simmer for 25 minutes.

Place ½ cup of the bean mixture in a blender and blend until smooth. Return puree to dutch oven and cook, uncovered, for 5 minutes more. Remove from heat, stir in remaining oil, and let stand, uncovered, for 10 minutes to thicken slightly. Flavors improve if soup is refrigerated overnight or for at least 4 hours. Reheat over medium heat.

Makes 6–7 cups

SUGGESTED GARNISH: Diced avocado, finely chopped Anaheim chile, and lime wedges

Roasted Red and Yellow Pepper Soup

A spectacular, highly flavored creamed chile soup, this features an exciting blend of roasted sweet yellow and red peppers, cayenne, and half-and-half.

3 medium-size yellow bell peppers
3 medium-size red bell peppers
3 cups canned chicken broth (not condensed)
1 cup chopped yellow onion
½ cup chopped celery
½ teaspoon cayenne pepper
2 cups half-and-half
Salt to taste

Preheat broiler. Cut peppers in half lengthwise, remove stems, seeds, and membranes, and flatten with your palm. Place cut-side down on a foil-lined oven rack and broil 2–3 inches from heat source for 7 minutes or until completely blistered, turning occasionally. Transfer to a bowl of ice water and let stand for 5 minutes.

Peel peppers and place in a dutch oven. Add broth, onion, celery, and cayenne and bring to a boil over high heat. Reduce heat to low and simmer, uncovered, for 15 minutes. Remove from heat, transfer 1 cup of the mixture to a blender, and blend until completely smooth. Transfer to a large bowl and repeat until all the soup is pureed.

Return puree to dutch oven, add half-and-half, and bring to a simmer over medium heat. Simmer until thickened, about 5–10 minutes. Add salt to taste before serving. Flavors will be at their peak if the soup is served immediately.

Makes about 6 cups

Suggested garnish: Small whole green jalapeño chiles surrounded by finely chopped red bell pepper

Cook's Note: The soup can be made up to 8 hours in advance, and refrigerated, without the half-and-half. At serving time, reheat over medium heat, slowly whisk in half-and-half, and simmer for 5–10 minutes.

Creamy Garbanzo Chipotle Soup*

Garbanzo beans and browned onions are infused with the smoky heat of chiles and pureed to a creamy consistency.

- 1 dried chipotle chile
- 1 cup boiling water
- 2 15-ounce cans garbanzo beans, rinsed and drained
- 2 tablespoons extra-virgin olive oil
- 4 garlic cloves, peeled
- 2 cups chopped yellow onion
- 2 14½-ounce cans beef broth (not condensed)

Place chile in a bowl, cover with boiling water, and let stand for 30 minutes to rehydrate.

While chile is soaking, place beans on paper towels, pat dry, and set aside. Place oil in a dutch oven (preferably cast iron) and heat over medium-high heat for 1 minute. Add garlic and onion and cook for 5–6 minutes or until edges of onion begin to brown. Add the beans to the garlic and onions and sauté about 8–10 minutes. Add all but 1 cup of the broth to beans, bring to a boil, reduce heat to low, and simmer, uncovered, for 10 minutes.

Remove chipotle chile from water (discard water). Wearing rubber or plastic gloves, remove stem, seeds, and membranes. Place chile in a blender with remaining cup of broth and process until smooth (about 2–3 minutes). Stir into bean mixture.

One cup at a time, transfer bean mixture to blender and process until very smooth. Return to dutch oven, bring to a simmer over medium heat, and simmer for 10 minutes. If a thinner consistency is desired, add ½ cup hot water before serving. Flavors improve if soup is refrigerated overnight or for at least 4 hours. Reheat over low heat.

Makes about 4 cups

SUGGESTED GARNISH:
Sour cream, coarsely ground black pepper, and small whole red jalapeños

Pinto Bean and Jalapeño Soup

A creamed pinto bean soup with onions, green chiles, tomatoes, seasonings, and fresh lime juice, this dish is served with tortilla chips, sour cream, scallions, fresh tomatoes, and cheddar cheese.

1 tablespoon extra-virgin olive oil
2 cups chopped yellow onion
2 15-ounce cans pinto beans, rinsed and drained
4 jalapeño chiles, seeded
2 tablespoons chili powder
1 tablespoon ground cumin
1 14½-ounce can diced tomatoes, undrained
1 4-ounce can green chiles, rinsed and drained
1 10-ounce can condensed beef broth
½ cup water
1 teaspoon ground coriander
¼ teaspoon black pepper
¼ teaspoon cayenne pepper
1 tablespoon fresh lime juice

GARNISHES

Tortilla chips
Sour cream
Chopped scallions
Chopped tomatoes
Grated sharp cheddar cheese

Place oil in a dutch oven (preferably cast iron) and heat over medium-high heat for 1 minute. Add onion and cook for 4 minutes or until translucent. Add remaining ingredients except lime juice and garnishes. Bring to a boil, reduce heat, and simmer, uncovered, for 20 minutes. Remove from heat.

One cup at a time, transfer soup to a blender and blend until smooth. Return puree to dutch oven and reheat over medium heat for about 5 minutes. Stir in lime juice immediately and serve with tortilla chips topped with a dollop of sour cream, scallion, chopped tomatoes, and cheddar cheese.

Makes about 5 cups

Rich Corn and Green Chile Soup with Cheddar Cheese

Sweet yellow corn, roasted Anaheim and poblano chiles, onions, and garlic are simmered gently in chicken broth with half-and-half and cheddar cheese.

- 2 fresh Anaheim or New Mexican green chiles
- 2 fresh poblano chiles
- 2 tablespoons butter
- 1 cup chopped yellow onion
- 4 garlic cloves, minced
- 1 14½-ounce can chicken broth (not condensed)
- 4 cups fresh or frozen corn kernels
- 1 cup half-and-half
- 1½ cups (about 6 ounces) shredded sharp cheddar cheese (Monterey Jack may be substituted if desired)

Preheat broiler. Place Anaheim and poblano chiles on a foil-lined oven rack and broil 2–3 inches from heat source for 10–12 minutes or until completely blistered, turning occasionally. Transfer to a bowl of ice water and let stand for 5 minutes. Peel chiles, remove stems, seeds, and membranes, chop, and set aside.

Place butter in a dutch oven (preferably cast iron) and heat over medium heat until melted and beginning to bubble. Add onion, garlic, and chopped chiles and cook for 4 minutes or until onion is translucent. Add broth and corn and bring to a boil. Reduce heat, cover tightly, and simmer for 15 minutes. Remove from heat, slowly whisk in half-and-half, add cheese, and stir to melt. Cover and let stand for 10 minutes before serving. Reheat over low heat.

Makes about 6 cups

Suggested garnish:
Chili powder

Index

▼▼▼

About the Author

▼▼▼

Nancy S. Hughes, a member of the International Association of Culinary Professionals, is the author of six cookbooks, including *The Four-Course 400-Calorie Cookbook*, *The 300-Calorie One-Dish Meal Cookbook*, and the *1200-Calorie-a-Day Menu Cookbook*. Her articles have appeared in *Cooking Light*, *Pillsbury's Fast and Healthy*, and other magazines. A cooking instructor who teaches and lectures at various medical, professional, business, and social organizations, Ms. Hughes resides in Daphne, Alabama, with her husband and three children.